TEACHER'S PET PUBLICATIONS

LITPLAN TEACHER PACK
for
The Light in the Forest
based on the book by
Conrad Richter

Written by
Barbara M. Linde, MA Ed.

© 1995 Teacher's Pet Publications
All Rights Reserved

This **LitPlan** for Conrad Richter's
The Light in the Forest
has been brought to you by Teacher's Pet Publications, Inc.

Copyright Teacher's Pet Publications 1995
11504 Hammock Point
Berlin MD 21811

Only the student materials in this unit plan (such as worksheets, study questions, and tests) may be reproduced multiple times for use in the purchaser's classroom.

For any additional copyright questions,
contact Teacher's Pet Publications.

www.tpet.com

TABLE OF CONTENTS - *The Light in the Forest*

Introduction	5
Unit Objectives	7
Unit Outline	8
Reading Assignment Sheet	9
Study Questions	13
Quiz/Study Questions (Multiple Choice)	21
Pre-Reading Vocabulary Worksheets	47
Lesson One (Introductory Lesson)	57
Nonfiction Assignment Sheet	60
Oral Reading Evaluation Form	63
Writing Assignment 1	65
Writing Evaluation Form	66
Writing Assignment 2	69
Extra Writing Assignments/Discussion ?s	72
Writing Assignment 3	76
Vocabulary Review Activities	77
Unit Review Activities	80
Unit Tests	85
Unit Resource Materials	125
Vocabulary Resource Materials	141

A FEW NOTES ABOUT THE AUTHOR
CONRAD RICHTER

RICHTER, Conrad Michael 1890-1968 Conrad Richter was born on October 13, 1890, in Pine Grove, Pennsylvania. He started working when he was fifteen. His early jobs included teamster, clerk, farm hand, and bank teller. At nineteen he became the editor of the weekly *Courier* in Patton, Pennsylvania. After that he worked as a reporter at newspapers in Pittsburgh and Johnstown, Pennsylvania. In 1928 Richter moved to the West and began a career as a full-time writer, specializing in fictional accounts of early American life.

The Trees, 1940, *The Fields*, 1946, and *The Town*, 1950, are probably Richter's best known works. The three novels deal realistically with early American life on the frontier. Richter enjoys looking into the minds of the pioneers as well as the myths about their life. His other writings include *Brothers of No Kin, and Other Stories*, 1924; *Early Americana and Other Stories*, 1936; *The Sea of Grass*, 1937; *Tacey Cromwell*, 1942; *The Light in the Forest*, 1953; *The Mountain on the Desert*, 1955; *Over the Blue Mountain*, 1962; *The Wanderer*, 1966; and *The Aristocrat*, 1966. *The Sea of Grass* was made into a movie in 1947 by MGM. *The Light in the Forest* was filmed in 1958 by Buena Vista (Walt Disney Productions.) The novel *Tacey Cromwell* was the basis for the Universal film "One Desire" in 1955.

Richter was the recipient of many literary awards throughout his career. In 1942 he was awarded the Gold Medal for Literature of Society of Libraries of New York University for *Sea of Grass* and *The Trees*. In 1951 he was awarded the Ohioana Library Medal. Richter received the 1951 Pulitzer Prize for Fiction for *The Town*. He also received the National Institute of Arts and Letters grant in literature in 1959; the Maggie Award in 1959 for *The Lady*; and the National Book Award in 1961 for *The Waters of Kronos*. His honorary degrees include Litt. D., Susquehanna University, 1944, University of New Mexico, 1958, Lafayette College, 1966; LL.D., Temple University, 1966; and L.H.D., Lebanon Valley College, 1966.

INTRODUCTION

This unit has been designed to develop students' reading, writing, thinking, listening and speaking skills through exercises and activities related to *The Light in the Forest* by Conrad Richter. It includes eighteen lessons, supported by extra resource materials.

The **introductory lesson** introduces students to one main theme of the novel, in order to attain what the white man thought of as civilization, he gave up many liberties, through a bulletin board activity. Following the introductory activity, students are given an explanation of how the activity relates to the book they are about to read.

The **reading assignments** are approximately twenty pages each; some are a little shorter while others are a little longer. Students have approximately 15 minutes of pre-reading work to do prior to each reading assignment. This pre-reading work involves reviewing the study questions for the assignment and doing some vocabulary work for 10 to 15 vocabulary words they will encounter in their reading.

The **study guide questions** are fact-based questions; students can find the answers to these questions right in the text. These questions come in two formats: short answer or multiple choice. The best use of these materials is probably to use the short answer version of the questions as study guides for students (since answers will be more complete), and to use the multiple choice version for occasional quizzes. It might be a good idea to make transparencies of your answer keys for the overhead projector.

The **vocabulary work** is intended to enrich students' vocabularies as well as to aid in the students' understanding of the book. Prior to each reading assignment, students will complete a two-part worksheet for approximately 10 to 15 vocabulary words in the upcoming reading assignment. Part I focuses on students' use of general knowledge and contextual clues by giving the sentence in which the word appears in the text. Students are then to write down what they think the words mean based on the words' usage. Part II gives students dictionary definitions of the words and has them match the words to the correct definitions based on the words' contextual usage. Students should then have an understanding of the words when they meet them in the text.

After each reading assignment, students will go back and formulate answers for the study guide questions. Discussion of these questions serves as a **review** of the most important events and ideas presented in the reading assignments.

After students complete extra discussion questions, there is a **vocabulary review** lesson which pulls together all of the separate vocabulary lists for the reading assignments and gives students a review of all of the words they have studied.

Following the reading of the book, two lessons are devoted to the **extra discussion questions/writing assignments**. These questions focus on interpretation, critical analysis and personal response, employing a variety of thinking skills and adding to the students' understanding of the novel. These questions are done as a **group activity**. Using the information they have acquired so far through individual work and class discussions, students get together to further examine the text and to brainstorm ideas relating to the themes of the novel.

The group activity is followed by a **reports and discussion** session in which the groups share their ideas about the book with the entire class; thus, the entire class gets exposed to many different ideas regarding the themes and events of the book.

There are three **writing assignments** in this unit, each with the purpose of informing, persuading, or having students express personal opinions. The first assignment is to **inform**: students will pretend to be early settlers in the Pennsylvania-Ohio area and write a letter describing their life to a friend in England. The second assignment is to **persuade**: students will take a position either in favor of or against returning the Indians' captives to their white relatives, and attempt to persuade the other side to agree with them. The third assignment is to express a personal **opinion**: students will describe their ideas about freedom.

In addition, there is a **nonfiction reading assignment**. Students are required to read a piece of nonfiction related in some way to *The Light in the Forest*. After reading their nonfiction pieces, students will fill out a worksheet on which they answer questions regarding facts, interpretation, criticism, and personal opinions. During one class period, students make **oral presentations** about the nonfiction pieces they have read. This not only exposes all students to a wealth of information, it also gives students the opportunity to practice **public speaking**.

The **review lesson** pulls together all of the aspects of the unit. The teacher is given four or five choices of activities or games to use which all serve the same basic function of reviewing all of the information presented in the unit.

The **unit test** comes in two formats: all multiple choice-matching-true/false or with a mixture of matching, short answer, and composition. As a convenience, two different tests for each format have been included.

There are additional **support materials** included with this unit. The **extra activities packet** includes suggestions for an in-class library, crossword and word search puzzles related to the novel, and extra vocabulary worksheets. There is a list of **bulletin board ideas** which gives the teacher suggestions for bulletin boards to go along with this unit. In addition, there is a list of **extra class activities** the teacher could choose from to enhance the unit or as a substitution for an exercise the teacher might feel is inappropriate for his/her class. **Answer keys** are located directly after the **reproducible student materials** throughout the unit. The student materials may be reproduced for use in the teacher's classroom without infringement of copyrights. No other portion of this unit may be reproduced without the written consent of Teacher's Pet Publications, Inc.

UNIT OBJECTIVES *The Light in the Forest*

1. Through reading *The Light in the Forest,* students will analyze characters and their situations to better understand the themes of the novel.

2. Students will demonstrate their understanding of the text on four levels: factual, interpretive, critical, and personal.

3. Students will practice reading aloud and silently to improve their skills in each area.

4. Students will enrich their vocabularies and improve their understanding of the autobiography through the vocabulary lessons prepared for use in conjunction with it.

5. Students will answer questions to demonstrate their knowledge and understanding of the main events and characters in *The Light in the Forest.*

6. Students will practice writing through a variety of writing assignments.

7. The writing assignments in this are geared to several purposes:
    a. To check the students' reading comprehension;
    b. To make students think about the ideas presented by the novel;
    c. To make students put those ideas into perspective;
    d. To encourage critical and logical thinking;
    e. To provide the opportunity to practice good grammar and improve students' use of the English language.

8. Students will read aloud, report, and participate in large and small group discussions to improve their public speaking and personal interaction skills.

UNIT OUTLINE *The Light in the Forest.*

1 Unit Intro Distribute Unit Materials PV 1-3	2 Read 1-3 Study ?? 1-3	3 PVR 4-6 Oral Reading Evaluation	4 Quiz 1-6 PVR 7-8	5 Writing Assignment #1
6 Study ?? 7-8 PVR 9-11	7 Study ?? 9-11 Quiz 7-11 PVR 12-13	8 Study ?? 12-13 Writing Assignment #2	9 Writing Conference	10 PVR 14-15 Study ?? 14-15
11 Extra Discussion ??	12 Writing Assignment #3	13 Library Work	14 Vocabulary Review	15 Group Work
16 Non-Fiction Assignment	17 Review	18 Test		

Key: P = Preview Study Questions   V = Vocabulary Work   R = Read

READING ASSIGNMENT SHEET *The Light in the Forest*

Date to be Assigned	Chapters	Completion Date
	Chapters 1-3	
	Chapters 4-6	
	Chapters 7-8	
	Chapters 9-11	
	Chapters 12-13	
	Chapters 14-15	

STUDY QUESTIONS

SHORT ANSWER STUDY GUIDE QUESTIONS *The Light in the Forest*

Chapters 1-3
1. What news did True Son hear at the opening of the story?
2. How did True Son feel about the news? What did he do to show how he felt?
3. What did Cuyloga do about the decree?
4. According to Del, how did the Indians feel about giving up their white prisoners?
5. According to Del, what surprised the white soldier the most when they witnessed the Indians giving up their white captives?
6. What plan did True Son think of to keep from returning to Pennsylvania, and was it successful?
7. What helped to keep True Son's spirits up along the journey?

Chapters 4-6
1. What observations did True Son, Half Arrow, and Little Crane make about the white men?
2. What message did True Son give Half Arrow to relate to Cuyloga?
3. How did True Son know when he had entered the land of the white men?
4. Describe True Son's reactions when he first met his white father.
5. Why was Del sent with the boy?
6. What word that True Son's white father said caused a reaction in him, and why?
7. Describe the meeting between True Son and his white mother.
8. What kind of relationship did True Son and his white brother, Gordie, begin to develop?

Chapters 7-8
1. How did True Son feel as he lay in the bedroom?
2. What was the "Peshtank story," and how did True Son feel about it?
3. How was True Son "thrice imprisoned?"
4. What was Uncle Wilse's attitude about True Son being reassimilated into the white culture?
5. What did Uncle Wilse say about the killing and torturing of the Conestogo Indians?
6. What did Uncle George try to explain to True Son about the relationship between the whites and the Indians?
7. Why did True Son begin wearing white man's clothes?
8. How did the author describe True Son's perception of the life and customs of the white man?
9. What did Bejance say about himself and True Son in relation to the white folks?
10. Describe True Son's journey to look for Corn Blade.

Short Answer Study Guide Questions *The Light in the Forest* Page 2

Chapters 9-11
1. Whom did Aunt Kate invite to the house, and why?
2. What was True Son's main objection to Parson Elder?
3. Briefly summarize what Parson Elder told Johnny.
4. What advice did Parson Elder give to Myra and Aunt Kate?
5. What were Dr. Childsley's thoughts about True Son's illness?
6. What did True Son do after Gordie told him Aunt Kate had seen an Indian looking in the kitchen window?
7. Where did the two boys go, and why?

Chapters 12-13
1. What was the boys' plan?
2. What was True Son's only regret?
3. What did the boys do when they reached the Alleghi Sipu river?
4. How did their journey change after they passed Fort Pitt?
5. Describe True Son's homecoming.

Chapters 14-15
1. What did Little Crane's male relatives want to do, and why?
2. Why did Cuyloga think True Son should accompany him and the other men?
3. What was the cause of the conflict between Thitpan and True Son?
4. What was strange about True Son's dream that night?
5. What was True Son's role in the next stage of the raid?
6. How did True Son perform his duty?
7. What was the significance of True Son's half black-half white face?
8. What did Cuyloga do when it was his turn to vote?
9. What did Cuyloga tell True Son?
10. Describe the parting scene between Cuyloga and True Son.

SHORT ANSWER STUDY GUIDE QUESTIONS WITH ANSWERS *The Light in the Forest*

<u>Chapters 1-3</u>

1. What news did True Son hear at the opening of the story?
   He heard that the white prisoners the Indians had been capturing for many years were to be given back to the white people.

2. How did True Son feel about the news? What did he do to show how he felt?
   He didn't want to give up his Indian life. He ran away from the village, blackened his face, and hid in a hollow tree.

3. What did Cuyloga do about the decree?
   He tied True Son's hands and led him to the council house of the whites. He whispered to True Son to go like an Indian and not give him (Cuyloga) any shame.

4. According to Del, how did the Indians feel about giving up their white prisoners?
   He said they hated to give up the prisoners, whom they had adopted into their tribes. However, they hated even more the sight of white men settling in the area. The Indians were afraid the white men were taking over the country.

5. According to Del, what surprised the white soldier the most when they witnessed the Indians giving up their white captives?
   The men couldn't believe that many of the captives didn't want to go back to the whites.

6. What plan did True Son think of to keep from returning to Pennsylvania, and was it successful?
   He planned to eat some May apple root and kill himself. He was not able to do so while Del was guarding him. Then, while walking, he forgot to look for it because he was distracted by Half Arrow's company.

7. What helped to keep True Son's spirits up along the journey?
   His cousin, Half Arrow, accompanied him. Half Arrow had also brought True Son's bear skin from his father, new moccasins from his mother and sisters, and parched corn from his uncle.

Chapters 4-6

1. What observations did True Son, Half Arrow, and Little Crane make about the white men?
   Little Crane said they acted queerly because they were not an original people. They were foolish and troublesome because they were a mixed people, with different colored hair and dyes. They needed a Good Book from the Great Being to teach them good and bad. Half Arrow thought they were all near-sighted because they crowd close to stare at Indians. True Son thought they were hard of hearing because they talked so loudly. Little Crane thought they were young and heedless like children because they accumulated so many possessions. They all agreed that the white men were foolish in the woods.

2. What message did True Son give Half Arrow to relate to Cuyloga?
   True Son said he would bear his disgrace like an Indian and wait until the right time to strike.

3. How did True Son know when he had entered the land of the white men?
   He saw where the Indian forest had been destroyed and the white men's houses and farms built.

4. Describe True Son's reactions when he first met his white father.
   True Son was sure he had nothing in common with the man. He compared the white man unfavorably to his Indian father.

5. Why was Del sent with the boy?
   He was being sent as a translator. True Son suspected he was also being sent as a guard.

6. What word that True Son's white father said caused a reaction in him, and why?
   The word "Susquehanna" caused True Son to say, in the Delaware language, that he had heard his Indian father tell stories of how the white men stole the river and the graves of their ancestors.

7. Describe the meeting between True Son and his white mother.
   Myra Butler called him John, and said she was glad he was home. She told him he had to make up for lost time, and continue his education. She gave him pants and a jacket that had belonged to his white cousin.

8. What kind of relationship did True Son and his white brother, Gordie, begin to develop?
   They began to develop a relationship of mutual respect and understanding.

Chapters 7-8

1. How did True Son feel as he lay in the bedroom?
   He felt sealed up as in a grave.

2. What was the "Peshtank story," and how did True Son feel about it?
   One December, a group of Conestogo Indians who had converted to Christianity were massacred by a group of white men from Paxton, or "Peshtank." Remembering the story filled True Son with hate.

3. How was True Son "thrice imprisoned?"
   He was imprisoned by being in the alien land, Yengue house, and white boy's clothes.

4. What was Uncle Wilse's attitude about True Son being reassimilated into the white culture?
   He thought True Son still looked more Indian. He said True Son had been brought up as an Indian and would stay that way.

5. What did Uncle Wilse say about the killing and torturing of the Conestogo Indians?
   He said they deserved it. He said the white men had to make sure the Indian males didn't kill any more whites, and the Indian females didn't have any more children. Later he said he believed in getting rid of vermin.

6. What did Uncle George try to explain to True Son about the relationship between the whites and the Indians?
   He felt the whites in the wilderness had to take the law into their own hands. If a white man killed an Indian, the trial was usually moved to Philadelphia, where the white man was convicted and hanged. However, if an Indian killed a white man, sympathizers in Bucks County or Philadelphia would shelter the Indian.

7. Why did True Son begin wearing white man's clothes?
   Aunt Kate took his Indian clothes and moccasins one night while he was asleep.

8. How did the author describe True Son's perception of the life and customs of the white man?
   He said it was like a plague.

9. What did Bejance say about himself and True Son in relation to the white folks?
   He said they would never be free from the whites. The whites would gradually strap them in until they hardly noticed they weren't free anymore.

10. Describe True Son's journey to look for Corn Blade.
    Gordie asked to go with him. They took a horse and some supplies. They were recognized when they passed Uncle Wilse's house. His father and Uncle Wilse came after them and made them return to the house.

Chapters 9-11
1. Whom did Aunt Kate invite to the house, and why?
    She invited Parson Elder. She felt he was responsible for bringing Johnny home, since he had led the prayers that had been answered. She was not happy with the way Johnny was acting. She wanted the Parson to talk to him.

2. What was True Son's main objection to Parson Elder?
    True Son knew that Parson Elder had been one of the leaders of the Peshtank men.

3. Briefly summarize what Parson Elder told Johnny.
    He said that there were some evil whites, but that he just wanted a friendship. He said that sometimes even good Christians got out of hand. He defended his actions by saying the Peshtank men had threatened to kill his favorite horse if he persisted in trying to stop the fighting.

4. What advice did Parson Elder give to Myra and Aunt Kate?
    He told them to be patient and guide Johnny, but not to push him. He also said that if Johnny found a pretty girl he would probably settle down.

5. What were Dr. Childsley's thoughts about True Son's illness?
    He was not able to diagnose it. He thought it was some Indian ailment that white doctors didn't know about. He thought the fever was probably a result of True Son's long and unhappy captivity.

6. What did True Son do after Gordie told him Aunt Kate had seen an Indian looking in the kitchen window?
    He waited until Gordie went to sleep, then climbed out the window. He found Half Arrow in the woods.

7. Where did the two boys go, and why?
    They went to Uncle Wilse's cooperage because Little Crane had been killed there. They attacked Uncle Wilse and tried, unsuccessfully, to scalp him. Then they went to the Butler's barn and True Son collected the article he had been hiding. The two ran away.

Chapters 12-13
1. What was the boys' plan?
    They were planning to walk back to their home on the Tuscarawas.

2. What was True Son's only regret?
    He regretted leaving Gordie.

3. What did the boys do when they reached the Alleghi Sipu river?
    Half Arrow stole a boat and they floated in it past Fort Pitt and into the Ohio River.

4. How did their journey change after they passed Fort Pitt?
    They were not afraid of being discovered by the whites, and became freer and less cautious in their actions. They spent about two months hunting, fishing, and relaxing.

5. Describe True Son's homecoming.
    When they reached the Muskingum river they bathed in it. When they reached the village, True Son walked past his sisters and his mother and embraced his father.

Chapters 14-15
1. What did Little Crane's male relatives want to do, and why?
    Thitpan, Little Crane's brother, wanted to avenge his brother's death by killing whites.

2. Why did Cuyloga think True Son should accompany him and the other men?
    He told his wife the other warriors would think True Son was unwilling to fight against his white people if he did not go.

3. What was the cause of the conflict between Thitpan and True Son?
    True Son knew that one of the scalps belonged to a child. When he brought the matter up to Thitpan, he was met with disapproval by the others.

4. What was strange about True Son's dream that night?
    He dreamed about his white parents.

5. What was True Son's role in the next stage of the raid?
    He was to look like a white boy in order to decoy a white flatboat on the river. The Indians wanted it to come close enough to the shore for the Indians to capture it.

6. How did True Son perform his duty?

    He failed. He saw a small boy on the boat who reminded him of his white brother, Gordie. He called to the people on the boat that they were about to be ambushed. The boat pulled away and the Indians were unable to capture it.

7. What was the significance of True Son's half black-half white face?

    The council was undecided about what to do with him. The charcoal signified death and the clay signified life.

8. What did Cuyloga do when it was his turn to vote?

    He took a stick from the fire and blackened his entire face. He told the others that he was responsible for True Son's bad instruction and should be burned as well.

9. What did Cuyloga tell True Son?

    He said True Son's heart and head were Indian, but his blood was still thin like the whites. He said he would take True Son to a white man's road, and they would part there. After that, they would no longer be father and son.

10. Describe the parting scene between Cuyloga and True Son.

    When they reached the white man's trail, True Son asked his father to say good- by. Cuyloga replied that enemies did not say good by, that they were no longer father and son. True Son asked who his father was, but received no answer.

MULTIPLE CHOICE STUDY GUIDE/QUIZ QUESTIONS *The Light in the Forest*

Chapters 1-3
1. What news did True Son hear at the opening of the story?
   A. The whites and Indians were going to sign a peace treaty.
   B. The white prisoners the Indians had captured were to be returned to the whites.
   C. The Indians were to be relocated to a reservation in the far west.
   D. The leader of his tribe had converted to Christianity and ordered the others to do so.

2. How did True Son feel about the news? What did he do to show how he felt?
   A. He didn't want to give up his Indian life. He ran away from the village, blackened his face, and hid in a hollow tree.
   B. He was happy about it. He started dancing and singing in English.
   C. He was not happy, but he was resigned to it. He packed the things he wanted to take with him, and gave the rest to his sisters and his cousins.
   D. He didn't want to go. He cried and begged Cuyloga not to send him.

3. What did Cuyloga do about the decree?
   A. He said he would never give up his son. He threatened to start a war if the white men came to get the captives.
   B. He said he would leave the decision up to True Son.
   C. He said he was glad to give up True Son if it would keep the peace between the Indians and the whites. He gave True Son new clothes to wear on the journey.
   D. He tied True Son's hands and led him to the council house of the whites. He whispered to True Son to go like an Indian and not give him (Cuyloga) any shame.

4. True or False: According to Del, the Indians were glad to get rid of them because most of them had been more trouble than they were worth.
   A. True
   B. False

5. According to Del, what surprised the white soldier the most when they witnessed the Indians giving up their white captives?
   A. The white captives looked healthy and well taken care of.
   B. Most of the captives were children.
   C. Many of the captives didn't want to go back to the whites.
   D. The Indians were crying and holding on to the captives.

Multiple Choice Study Guide/Quiz Questions *The Light in the Forest* 1-3 Continued

6. What plan did True Son think of to keep from returning to Pennsylvania?
   A. He planned to eat some May apple root and kill himself.
   B. He planned to grab Del's rifle and run away.
   C. He planned to pretend he was crazy so the whites would not want him.
   D. He planned to capture a younger child as hostage and escape into the woods.

7. What helped to keep True Son's spirits up along the journey?
   A. He sang traditional tribal songs to himself.
   B. He read a letter Cuyloga had given him just before he left.
   C. He constantly plotted ways of escaping.
   D. His cousin, Half Arrow, accompanied him.

Multiple Choice Study Guide/Quiz Questions *The Light in the Forest*

Chapters 4-6

1. True Son, Half Arrow, and Little Crane made some observations about the white men. Which of the following was **not** one of them?
   A. They acted queerly because they were not an original people.
   B. They were all far-sighted because they stood so far away from the Indians.
   C. They were hard of hearing because they talked so loudly.
   D. The white men were foolish in the woods

2. What message did True Son give Half Arrow to relate to Cuyloga?
   A. He would be home again in six moons or less.
   B. The tribe should not risk war to come for him.
   C. He would always be the True Son, and would never forget his Indian family.
   D. He would bear his disgrace like an Indian and wait until the right time to strike.

3. How did True Son know when he had entered the land of the white men?
   A. He saw road signs in a language he could not understand.
   B. There was a barbed wire fence across the trail that separated the two sides.
   C. He saw where the Indian forest had been destroyed and the white men's houses and farms built.
   D. There was a fort built on the edge of the white land. The group had to go through the fort and the prisoners had to be searched before they could go any further.

4. Describe True Son's reactions when he first met his white father.
   A. True Son turned away and refused to acknowledge the man as his father.
   B. True Son was sure he had nothing in common with the man. He compared the white man unfavorably to his Indian father.
   C. True Son laughed in the man's face and told him that a brave warrior like himself could not possibly be the son of such a cowardly looking man.
   D. True Son immediately saw a resemblance between himself and the white man, but he refused to admit it. He stood and glared at the man.

5. True or False: Del Hardy was being sent with the boy as a translator, but True Son suspected he was also being sent to guard him.
   A. True
   B. False

Multiple Choice Study Guide/Quiz Questions *The Light in the Forest* 4-6 Continued

6. What word that True Son's white father said caused a reaction in him, and why?
   A. The word "Susquehanna" caused True Son to say, in the Delaware language, that he had heard his Indian father tell stories of how the white men stole the river and the graves of their ancestors.
   B. The word "Muskingum" caused True Son to remember the stories about how the whites had captured the chief of the Muskingum and tortured him.
   C. The word "Cuyloga" made him realize the others were talking about his Indian father. He began to worry that they were planning something against him.
   D. The words "Fort Pitt" gave him a clue to their destination. He had heard that Fort Pitt was the largest building in the world. He was curious to see it.

7. Describe the meeting between True Son and his white mother.
   A. She got so upset at his Indian clothes and looks that she had to be given a sedative. True Son was taken to another room and told he would see her the next day.
   B. She called him John, and said she was glad he was home. She said he had to make up for lost time and continue his education. She gave him pants and a jacket to wear.
   C. She cried and hugged him. He remembered her, and hugged her in return.
   D. He refused to go in the room. She finally came out into the hallway, but he turned and ran down the stairs and out into the garden.

8. Which of the following statements is true about Gordie and True Son?
   A. Gordie was jealous of the attention True Son was getting.
   B. True Son found he could get the adults angry by teasing Gordie.
   C. Gordie asked True Son to take him back to the Indians to live.
   D. They began to develop a relationship of mutual respect and understanding.

Multiple Choice Study Guide/Quiz Questions *The Light in the Forest*

<u>Chapters 7-8</u>

1. How did True Son feel as he lay in the bedroom?
   A. He felt like an animal in a trap.
   B. He felt sealed up as in a grave.
   C. He felt like he had already died and gone to the underworld.
   D. He felt totally alone and forsaken by his God and his people.

2. True or False: The "Peshtank story" concerned a group of Conestogo Indians who had converted to Christianity. They were massacred by a group of white men from Paxton township.
   A. True
   B. False

3. How was True Son "thrice imprisoned?"
   A. He had no one to talk to in the Delaware language, he was not able to go outdoors, and he was wearing white men's clothes.
   B. He was chained to the bedpost, the door to his room was barred from the outside, and there was a guard under the window.
   C. He had to eat the white people's food, go to their church, and sleep in a bed.
   D. He was in the alien land, Yengue house, and white boy's clothes.

4. True or False: Uncle Wilse thought True Son looked white again. He said True Son had been baptized a Christian and that his first four years as a Christian would help him forget the Indian ways.
   A. True
   B. False

5. Who made the following statements about the killing and torturing of the Conestogo Indians? They deserved it. The white men had to make sure the Indian males didn't kill any more whites, and the Indian females didn't have any more children. It was right to get rid of vermin.
   A. Uncle Wilse
   B. Aunt Kate
   C. George Butler
   D. Del

Multiple Choice Study Guide/Quiz Questions *The Light in the Forest* 7-8 Continued

6. Uncle George said the whites in the wilderness had to take the law into their own hands. What was his reason for this statement?
   A. The whites were Christians and knew better how to tell right from wrong. They really only wanted to help the pagan Indians lead better lives.
   B. The cities where the judges lived were too far away to do them any good.
   C. The laws in Philadelphia and Bucks County were too sympathetic toward the Indians.
   D. They did not have enough money to pay for an army unit to guard them.

7. Why did True Son begin wearing white man's clothes?
   A. Gordie asked him to because he wanted them to be dressed alike.
   B. Aunt Kate took his Indian clothes and moccasins one night while he was asleep.
   C. He thought it would make him seem more trustworthy.
   D. His Indian clothes got too small.

8. How did the author describe True Son's perception of the life and customs of the white man?
   A. It was like a steel trap.
   B. It was like a stone around his neck.
   C. It was like being at the bottom of a well with no way up.
   D. It was like a plague.

9. What did Bejance say about himself and True Son in relation to the white folks?
   A. He said the white folks didn't really like either of them but would not admit it because they wanted to be thought of as good Christians.
   B. He said they were both better than the white folks, and they could show it in their daily actions.
   C. He said they would never be free from the whites. The whites would gradually strap them in until they hardly noticed they weren't free anymore.
   D. He said the white folks would eventually grow tired of fighting with the Indians and the Blacks and would leave them all alone.

10. Which of the following did **not** happen on True Son's journey to look for Corn Blade?
    A. True Son took Gordie along as a hostage.
    B. They took a horse and some supplies.
    C. They were recognized when they passed Uncle Wilse's house.
    D. His father and Uncle Wilse came after them and made them return to the house.

Multiple Choice Study Guide/Quiz Questions *The Light in the Forest*

<u>Chapters 9-11</u>

1. Why did Aunt Kate invite Parson Elder to the house?
    A. She invited him to comfort Mrs. Butler, who was ill with a high fever.
    B. She invited him to teach True Son to read the Bible.
    C. She invited him to talk to True Son about the way he was acting.
    D. She invited him teach True Son to dance in preparation for a party.

2. What was True Son's main objection to Parson Elder?
    A. He was a drunkard who always smelled of whiskey.
    B. He had been one of the leaders of the Peshtank men.
    C. He talked too much and didn't listen.
    D. He was totally ignorant of the ways of the Indians.

3. What was Parson Elder's defense of his actions with the Peshtank men?
    A. He believed they were on a holy mission from God and should not be stopped.
    B. They had threatened to kill his wife and children if he did not help them.
    C. The Indians had killed his parents and he wanted vengeance.
    D. They had threatened to kill his favorite horse if he tried to stop them.

4. True or False: Parson Elder told Myra and Aunt Kate to be patient and guide Johnny, but not to push him. He also said that if Johnny found a pretty girl he would probably settle down.
    A. True
    B. False

5. What were Dr. Childsley's thoughts about True Son's illness?
    A. He thought the fever was due to True Son's long and unhappy captivity.
    B. He thought True Son was faking to get attention from everyone.
    C. He thought True Son had eaten some May apples to try and kill himself.
    D. He thought True Son was not used to the good food and water the family gave him.

6. What did True Son do after Gordie told him Aunt Kate had seen an Indian looking in the kitchen window?
    A. He laughed and said Gordie was seeing things.
    B. He immediately went to the window and started shouting in Delaware for help.
    C. He waited until Gordie went to sleep, then climbed out the window.
    D. He ran down to the kitchen, stole a knife, and ran outside to look around.

Multiple Choice Study Guide/Quiz Questions *The Light in the Forest* 9-11 Continued

7. Which of the following was **not** one of the boys' actions?
   A. They went to the cooperage.
   B. They tried to scalp Uncle Wilse.
   C. True Son collected the article he had been hiding in his father's barn.
   D. They set the Butlers' house and barn on fire.

Multiple Choice Study Guide/Quiz Questions *The Light in the Forest*

Chapters 12-13

1. What was the boys' plan?
    A. They were planning to kill whites and destroy their property all over the area.
    B. They were planning to take white children captive and take them back to the Indians.
    C. They were planning to rescue the other whites who had been returned to their families.
    D. They were planning to walk back to their home on the Tuscarawas.

2. What was True Son's only regret?
    A. He regretted that Cuyloga could not see all the daring things he was doing.
    B. He regretted leaving Gordie.
    C. He regretted not stealing jewels and pretty ribbons to give his mother and sisters.
    D. He regretted not taking many scalps with them.

3. True or False: Half Arrow stole a boat and they floated in it past Fort Pitt and into the Ohio River.
    A. True
    B. False

4. True or False: Soldiers from Fort Pitt pursued the boys almost all the way back to the Tuscarawas.
    A. True
    B. False

5. Describe True Son's homecoming.
    A. True Son cried and danced from happiness. His father told him to be quiet and act like a dignified warrior.
    B. The other members of the tribe acted like he had never been gone. The tribal life went on as usual.
    C. The tribe held a great feast. His father performed a cleansing ritual to rid True Son of the white influences.
    D. When they reached the Muskingum river they bathed in it. When they reached the village, True Son walked past his sisters and his mother and embraced his father.

Multiple Choice Study Guide/Quiz Questions *The Light in the Forest*

Chapters 14-15

1. What did Little Crane's male relatives want to do, and why?
    A. High Bank, Little Crane's father-in-law, wanted to go to Uncle Wilse's farm and kill all of the people there.
    B. Niskitoon wanted to take their problems to the white man's court and ask them for justice.
    C. Thitpan, Little Crane's brother, wanted to avenge his brother's death by going to war against the white men.
    D. Cheek Bone wanted to capture a white man of Little Crane's age to take his place as husband and father for the family.

2. True or False: Cuyloga said True Son should accompany him and the other men so the other warriors would know he was willing to fight against his white people.
    A. True
    B. False

3. What was the cause of the conflict between Thitpan and True Son?
    A. True Son said his father should be the leader of the party since he knew the most about following the trails.
    B. Thitpan wanted True Son to walk ten paces behind the rest of the men because he was white, and not completely one of them. True Son insisted he was completely Indian.
    C. Thitpan wanted his family to get most of the booty. True Son thought it should be divided evenly.
    D. True Son knew that one of the scalps belonged to a child. When he brought the matter up to Thitpan, he was met with disapproval by the others.

4. What did True Son dream about that night?
    A. He dreamed about his white parents.
    B. He dreamed he was teaching Gordie to read and write in the Delaware language.
    C. He dreamed that Little Crane had come back to life as his Uncle Wilse.
    D. He dreamed he and Half Arrow were sledding on the hills near his white home.

Multiple Choice Study Guide/Quiz Questions *The Light in the Forest* 14-15 Continued

5. What was True Son's role in the next stage of the raid?
    A. He was to dress as a white boy and walk into the white camp. Once there, he was to steal guns and provisions and bring them back to the Indians.
    B. He was to look like a white boy in order to decoy a white flatboat on the river. The Indians wanted it to come close enough to the shore for the Indians to capture it.
    C. He was to lead the party on a raid of the nearby white village. He was to scalp as many children as possible.
    D. He was to lay on the trail and pretend to be wounded. When the white traders stopped to help, the other Indians would jump out of the bushes and kill them.

6. True or False: True Son failed in his duty. He saw a small boy who reminded him of his white brother, Gordie. He called to the people that they were about to be ambushed and they escaped.
    A. True
    B. False

7. What was the significance of True Son's half black-half white face?
    A. He was unsure about his identity. The black half symbolized his Indian side, and the clay represented his white side.
    B. The black side meant he would be left to die in the wilderness. The white meant he would be thrown into the river to drown.
    C. The black represented the evil in him. The clay represented the good. Whichever covering stayed on his face longer would show his true self. Then he would be punished accordingly.
    D. The council was undecided about what to do with him. The charcoal signified death and the clay signified life.

8. What did Cuyloga do when it was his turn to vote?
    A. He forced True Son to make the decision for him.
    B. He apologized to the group for taking a weak white boy as a son. He begged for forgiveness for the boy.
    C. He told the others that he was responsible for True Son's bad instruction, and should be burned as well.
    D. He told the others they should cut out True Son's tongue and blind him as punishment for being a liar and a spy.

Multiple Choice Study Guide/Quiz Questions *The Light in the Forest* 14-15 Continued

9. What did Cuyloga tell True Son?
   A. He told True Son to wait there in the woods. He said he would bring the family there and they would start their own tribe.
   B. He said True Son's heart and head were Indian, but his blood was thin like the whites. He said they would part at the white man's road, and no longer be father and son.
   C. He said True Son would be better off with the white people, but that he should never forget the ways of the Indians. He said he hoped they would meet again one day.
   D. He told True Son that since he had done wrong to the whites and the Indians, he would be doomed to travel alone for the rest of his life.

10. Describe the parting scene between Cuyloga and True Son.
    A. They both cried and hugged each other. Cuyloga said in his heart he would always be True Son's father. True Son said he would never feel at home among the white men, and would find a way to return to the Indians.
    B. True Son ran away into the woods before his father could say anything. Cuyloga left a gun, a blanket, and white man's clothes for True Son. Then he went back to the war party.
    C. True Son begged Cuyloga not to leave him. Cuyloga replied that he had no choice. If he did not leave the boy, the rest of the men would kill them both. He tried to assure True Son that they were better off this way.
    D. True Son asked his father to say good- by. Cuyloga replied that enemies did not say good by, that they were no longer father and son. True Son asked who his father was, but received no answer.

ANSWER KEY STUDY GUIDE MULTIPLE CHOICE/QUIZ QUESTIONS
The Light in the Forest

Chapters 1-3
1. B
2. A
3. D
4. B False
5. C
6. A
7. D

Chapters 4-6
1. B
2. D
3. C
4. B
5. A True
6. A
7. B
8. D

Chapters 7-8
1. B
2. A True
3. D
4. B False
5. A
6. C
7. B
8. D
9. C
10. A

Chapters 9-11
1. C
2. B
3. D
4. A True
5. A
6. C
7. D

Chapters 12-13
1. D
2. B
3. A True
4. B False
5. D

Chapters 14-15
1. C
2. A True
3. D
4. A
5. B
6. A True
7. D
8. C
9. B
10. D

PREREADING VOCABULARY WORKSHEETS

Chapters 1-3
Part I: Using Prior Knowledge and Context Clues

Below are the sentences in which the vocabulary words appear in the text. Read the sentence. Use any clues you can find in the sentence combined with your prior knowledge, and write what you think the underlined words mean on the lines provided.

1. It wasn't that he couldn't *endure* pain. In summer he would put a stone hot from the fire on his flesh to see how long he could stand it.

   _____

2. Then how could he be torn from his home like a *sapling* from the ground and given to the alien whites who were his enemy!

   _____

3. It was *humiliating* to be taken back with his blackened face and tied up in his father's cabin like some prisoner to be burned at the stake.

   _____

4. At the sight and smells of the white man, strong *aversion* and loathing came over him. He tried with all his young strength to get away.

   _____

5. At the sight and smells of the white man, strong aversion and *loathing* came over him. He tried with all his young strength to get away.

   _____

6. And now when they were so deep in Indian country it looked as if they'd never get out, the Colonel got *doughtier* and spunkier than ever. He sassed back the Indian messengers who came into the camp.

   _____

7. He had to be tied up with strips of buffalo hide, and then he struggled like a panther kit *trussed* up on a pole.

   _____

8. Now what did the young *varmint* mean by that, Del wondered.

   _____

9. The camp quickened. You could close your eyes and feel the nervous *bustle* and excitation of the white man.

   _____

10. Half Arrow ate greedily the bread True Son shared with him. At the same time he made a wry *grimace* over the meat. "What kind of flesh is this they give you?"

    _____

11. All afternoon the two cousins marched together, and at times True Son could almost forget the bitterness of his *destination*.

    _____

Part II: Determining the Meaning

____ 1.	endure	A.	twisting of the face that expresses pain or disgust
____ 2.	sapling	B.	the place to which one is going
____ 3.	humiliating	C.	a young tree
____ 4.	aversion	D.	to suffer patiently without yielding
____ 5.	loathing	E.	tied up
____ 6.	doughtier	F.	great dislike; abhorrence
____ 7.	trussed	G.	excited and often noisy activity; a stir
____ 8.	varmint	H.	extreme repugnance accompanied by avoidance
____ 9.	bustle	I.	one who is undesirable, obnoxious or troublesome
____ 10.	grimace	J.	more courageous
____ 11.	destination	K.	lowering the pride, dignity or self-respect of

Chapters 4-6
Part I: Using Prior Knowledge and Context Clues
Below are the sentences in which the vocabulary words appear in the text. Read the sentence. Use any clues you can find in the sentence combined with your prior knowledge, and write what you think the underlined words mean on the lines provided.

1. All the way to the _ominous_-sounding Fort Pitt, True Son tried to keep his mind from the gloomy hour when Half Arrow must turn back and leave him.

   _____

2. "The Great Being knows their _disposition_. He had to give them a Good Book and teach them to read so they could learn what is good and bad."

   _____

3. "They are young and _heedless_ like children, You can see it the way they heap up treasures like a child, although they know they must die and can't take such things with them."

   _____

4. "It is wiser to be willing and be alive than be _defiant_ and be dead so your father and mother and sisters have to mourn you."

   _____

5. From now forward he was on his own, the boy told himself. He would have to think his own Indian thoughts and follow his own _counsel_.

   _____

6. Here the _desolate_ face of the earth had been exposed to dead brown weeds and stubble, lorded over by the lodges of the white people and the fat storehouses of their riches.

   _____

7. The cattle stood tame and _stolid_ as the soldiers passed, but the white people came running from their lodges to line the road.

   _____

8. Here the whites had shut themselves up in prisons of gray stone and of red stone called brick, while the larger log houses had been covered over with smooth painted boards to give them the glittering *ostentation* and falseness so dear to the whites.

9. They were the captives' future masters, who could claim them and drag them off to a life of *subjegation* in their own lodges. Note: There appears to be a typographical error in some of the books. The correct spelling is *subjugation*.

10. How could this fantastic and inferior figure in a long fawn-colored garment like a woman's be possibly anything to him--this *pallid* creature who revealed his feelings in front of all!

11. No, the armed soldier was being sent along mostly to guard him, perhaps also to protect this slight *presumptuous* white man who claimed to be his father.

12. Yet, look at this Butler boy on ahead riding with his father, *sullen* as a young spider, making as though he didn't understand a word his father said.

13. True Son had wrapped himself again in *aloofness* like a blanket.

14. That broke the strain for a moment and all smiled, all except the boy in Indian dress. Gradually his insistent, *somber* silence overtook the others.

Part II: Determining the Meaning   Match the vocabulary words to their dictionary definitions.

_____ 1. ominous
_____ 2. disposition
_____ 3. heedless
_____ 4. defiant
_____ 5. counsel
_____ 6. desolate
_____ 7. stolid
_____ 8. ostentation
_____ 9. subjugation
_____ 10. pallid
_____ 11. presumptuous
_____ 12. sullen
_____ 13. aloofness
_____ 14. somber

A. not paying attention
B. revealing little emotion or sensibility; impassive
C. having an abnormally pale complexion
D. distant physically or emotionally; reserved
E. menacing; threatening
F. dark; gloomy
G. barren, lifeless
H. brooding; morose; sulky
I. one's usual mood; temperament
J. act of bringing under control; conquering
K. beyond what is right or proper; too forward
L. boldly resisting
M. boastful display to impress others; showiness
N. advice or guidance

Chapters 7-8
Part I: Using Prior Knowledge and Context Clues
Below are the sentences in which the vocabulary words appear in the text. Read the sentence. Use any clues you can find in the sentence combined with your prior knowledge, and write what you think the underlined words mean on the lines provided.

1. He could rise refreshed from a *suffocating* bed of feathers high as a turkey roost off his mother, the Earth.

   _____

2. He could still hear in his mind the "Peshtank story" that had swept through his village and the other Indian towns like a *pestilence*.

   _____

3. It gave him a feeling of *abhorrence*. Hardly could he bear even this white soldier, now in deep sleep beside him.

   _____

4. He felt *debased*. He was an Indian male obeying a white squaw, made to carry his with his own hands a bucket of steaming water up the stairs.

   _____

5. His only *consolation* was that his Indian father wasn't here to see.

   _____

6. Uncle Wilse had an expression of *derision*. "What does it matter what gibberish Indians talk?"

   _____

7. Uncle Wilse's face was *distorted*. He got halfway to his feet.

   _____

8. "No Indian friends of yours better come see you around here. If you expect that heathen *abductor* of yours, you better send him word to stay away."

   _____

9. That evening he pulled off the *tainted* clothes of his Cousin Alec and no one could induce him to let them touch his body again.

   _____

10. It was done, he suspected, so he wouldn't run away, for no man or boy could hope to get far through the woods in such *encumbrances*.

    _____

11. And now all the *odious* and joyless life of the white race, its incomprehensible customs and heavy ways, fell on him like a plague.

    _____

12. "You're not free like us," Gordie declared. "No. I'm never free from white folks," the Negro *assented*.

    _____

13. Like a half-grown panther playing at stalking its own den, he made his *stealthy* way to the barn.

    _____

Part II: Determining the Meaning   Match the vocabulary words to their dictionary definitions.

_____ 1. suffocating
_____ 2. pestilence
_____ 3. abhorrence
_____ 4. debased
_____ 5. consolation
_____ 6. derision
_____ 7. distorted
_____ 8. abductor
_____ 9. tainted
_____ 10. encumbrances
_____ 11. odious
_____ 12. assented
_____ 13. stealthy

A. a destructive, evil influence
B. acting with secrecy to avoid notice
C. relieving the sorrow or grief of
D. burdens or obstacles
E. kidnapper
F. a feeling of repugnance or loathing
G. agreed; concurred
H. lowered in character, quality, or value; degraded
I. ridicule
J. arousing strong dislike or intense displeasure
K. killing by taking away oxygen
L. twisted; misshapen
M. stained; infected; spoiled

Chapters 9-11
Part I: Using Prior Knowledge and Context Clues
Below are the sentences in which the vocabulary words appear in the text. Read the sentence. Use any clues you can find in the sentence combined with your prior knowledge, and write what you think the underlined words mean on the lines provided.

1. Most boys brought in front of the *formidable* Parson Elder were reluctant, some terrified, all uneasy. This boy stood before him without fear or inferiority.

   _____

2. "I've never seen it but I've heard of it and don't *condone* it."

   _____

3. "Well, I'm glad to hear such *precepts* from a pagan," the Reverend Elder said with dignity and just a little sarcasm.

   _____

4. "Sometimes even the most *exemplary* Christians get out of hand."

   _____

5. Aunt Kate had stepped up quickly to stop the boy, but the parson *deterred* her.

   _____

6. "Living here near the frontier, we have our own particular trials and *tribulations*," he said.

   _____

7. Indians were liable to mysterious forest *miasmas,* he said, and at times they died like pigeons.

   _____

8. Just the same if he bared his heart, it would relieve him and Johnny might bare his in return, expressing *filial* regret for his persistent and unhealthy passion for Indian ways and for his stubborn antagonism toward the decent thrifty ways of his white people.

9. Let her *hover* around for news.

10. A pity his eldest son hadn't been raised to evaluate and enjoy the satisfaction and benefits of honest work, the *solace* and support of ready cash, and the remuneration and accumulation of active property.

11. A pity his eldest son hadn't been raised to evaluate and enjoy the satisfaction and benefits of honest work, the solace and support of ready cash, and the *remuneration* and accumulation of active property.

12. But now he had stayed in the *insidious* company of white people too long. Their milkwarm water had gotten into his blood.

13. Later the white medicine man appeared, smelling of horses, practicing the white man's superstition of bleeding the feet and *purging* with powders.

14. From time to time he rested on the chair from his small *exertions*.

Part II: Determining the Meaning   Match the vocabulary words to their dictionary definitions.

_____ 1. formidable
_____ 2. condone
_____ 3. precepts
_____ 4. exemplary
_____ 5. deterred
_____ 6. tribulations
_____ 7. miasmas
_____ 8. filial
_____ 9. hover
_____ 10. solace
_____ 11. remuneration
_____ 12. insidious
_____ 13. purging
_____ 14. exertions

A. effort
B. comfort in trouble
C. great afflictions; suffering
D. rules or principles
E. purifying; cleansing
F. hang about; wait nearby
G. prevented or discouraged from acting
H. to overlook or forgive an offense without protest
I. intended to entrap; treacherous
J. pertaining to a son or daughter
K. worthy of being imitated
L. arousing fear, dread, or alarm
M. payment
N. swamp gases; odors of decaying matter

Chapters 12-13

Part I: Using Prior Knowledge and Context Clues

Below are the sentences in which the vocabulary words appear in the text. Read the sentence. Use any clues you can find in the sentence combined with your prior knowledge, and write what you think the underlined words mean on the lines provided.

1. He finished with *alacrity* and a flourish of drops.

   _____

2. The very breath of the path was Indian. It dipped through the dim *pungency* of pine groves where hardly would you know the season, and it broke out into the bright new greenness of the hardwoods where even the blind could tell that this was the Month When the Deer Turns Red.

   _____

3. But all the time he talked, Half Arrow kept to the path, *berating* the thieving whites, regretting there were only two against so many and that he and True Son would have so far to carry booty.

   _____

4. Never, True Son told his cousin, would he forget this morning in the Month When the Deer Turns Red, with the sight of Fort Pitt standing bristling on the point of land between the two rivers, its lights small and few, its strong stockade, redoubts and houses dark and *sinister* against the faint murky streaks of red and orange in the eastern sky.

   _____

5. All that day they drifted with the current, paddling a little from either shore where white landspies, traveling where they had no right, might *covet* their dugout.

   _____

6. Weaving them in and out of the branches, they tied each with a knot as it passed through. It took most of the hungry day. Then their brush *seine* was ready. . . . The little fish swam through it.

   _____

7. Always up to now they had gone as wards and *lackeys* of their fathers. Now at last they were their own masters.

_____

8. The sun had passed its northern *meridian* and was beginning its slow return.

_____

9. True Son looked at her with love and aloofness, carrying his rifle, passing her by, striding on with Half Arrow, past his older sister, Mechelit, who stood half-way with bright *vermilion* cloth in her black hair, on to the door of his cabin where his mother waited.

_____

10. Cuyloga's face was strong and impassive. Not a line could you read from its muscles, but from his eyes True Son thought he *discerned* a deep welcome.

_____

Part II: Determining the Meaning Match the vocabulary words to their dictionary definitions.

____	1. alacrity	A.	scolding
____	2. pungency	B.	speed or quickness
____	3. berating	C.	to want something that belongs to another
____	4. sinister	D.	slaves; forced laborers
____	5. covet	E.	a vivid red to reddish orange
____	6. seine	F.	stinging; capable of burning
____	7. lackeys	G.	net for catching fish
____	8. meridian	H.	evil
____	9. vermilion	I.	recognized or comprehended mentally
____	10. discerned	J.	highest point; peak

Chapters 14-15
Part I: Using Prior Knowledge and Context Clues
Below are the sentences in which the vocabulary words appear in the text. Read the sentence. Use any clues you can find in the sentence combined with your prior knowledge, and write what you think the underlined words mean on the lines provided.

1. With him were High Bank, his father-in-law, with only one eye; and Niskitoon, which means Put-on-Paint, whose skin was tattooed from head to foot with sighs of *valor*; also others, including Cheek Bone, a Shawano.

   _____

2. "The white man is a strange creature of the Almighty. He is hard to *fathom*. How can you reason with him?"

   _____

3. "I go!" True Son said quickly. He felt the flush of a great *exultation.*

   _____

4. The whole course of the stratagem was recounted, every sign and movement, the successful deception and ambush, all the fearful and cowardly efforts of the whites to escape and *appease* them, together with the foolish and fruitless words they cried in their religion which was no help to them now.

   _____

5. In the morning, Thitpan and Disbeliever instructed the boy in the *meritorious* art of decoy.

   _____

6. Surely some should be *allotted* to him, for without him the others could do nothing.

   _____

7. He called so piteously now that he could hear the voice of one of the women *remonstrating* with the unwilling men.

   _____

8. He couldn't make out the words, but her tone had the same *imperial* quality of his white mother when she forced her wishes on his white father.

   _____

9. For a moment the men on the boat stood startled. True Son saw terror and *incredulity* on the face of the white woman.

   _____

10. What they might do to his father in ambush later, he could not guess, but there would be no attempt to *molest* either of them now.

    _____

11. His father spoke *bleakly*. "This is the parting place. This is where the path must be closed between us."

    _____

12. Ahead of him ran the rutted road of the whites. It led, he knew, to where men of their own *volition* constrained themselves with heavy clothing like harness, where men chose to be slaves to their own or another's property and followed empty and desolate lives far from the wild beloved freedom of the Indian.

    _____

Part II: Determining the Meaning Match the vocabulary words to their dictionary definitions.

_____	1. valor	A.	gloomily; cheerlessly
_____	2. fathom	B.	deserving reward or praise
_____	3. exultation	C.	courage and boldness; bravery
_____	4. appease	D.	to disturb, interfere with, or annoy
_____	5. meritorious	E.	pleading in protest
_____	6. allotted	F.	a conscious choice or decision
_____	7. remonstrating	G.	unbelievable
_____	8. imperial	H.	pacify; soothe
_____	9. incredulity	I.	understand
_____	10. molest	J.	having supreme authority
_____	11. bleakly	K.	rejoicing
_____	12. volition	L.	parceled out; distributed or apportioned

ANSWER KEY-PREREADING VOCABULARY WORKSHEETS
The Light in the Forest

Chapters 1-3
1. D
2. C
3. K
4. H
5. F
6. J
7. E
8. I
9. G
10. A
11. B

Chapters 4-6
1. E
2. I
3. A
4. L
5. N
6. G
7. B
8. M
9. J
10. C
11. K
12. H
13. D
14. F

Chapters 7-8
1. K
2. A
3. F
4. H
5. C
6. I
7. L
8. E
9. M
10. D
11. J
12. G
13. B

Chapters 9-11
1. L
2. H
3. D
4. K
5. G
6. C
7.
8. N
9. J
10. F
11. M
12. I
13. E
14. A

Chapters 12-13
1. B
2. F
3. A
4. H
5. C
6. G
7. D
8. J
9. E
10. I

Chapters 14-15
1. C
2. I
3. K
4. H
5. B
6. L
7. E
8. J
9. G
10. D
11. A
12. F

DAILY LESSONS

LESSON ONE

Objectives
    1. To introduce the unit for *The Light in the Forest*
    2. To distribute books and other related materials (study guides, reading assignments)
    3. To relate students' prior knowledge to the new material
    4. To preview the study questions for Chapters 1-3
    5. To familiarize students with the vocabulary for Chapters 1-3

Activity #1

    Make a bulletin board display that includes the following items: a current map of Ohio and Pennsylvania, pictures of early (pre 1800s) white settlers, and pictures of Northeastern Indian tribes such as the Delaware. If possible, include a map of the Ohio and Pennsylvania area from the late 1700s. Tell students the setting of the story is what is now Ohio and Pennsylvania. Have them locate the Tuscarawas River in Ohio and trace it to the Ohio River in Pittsburgh, Pennsylvania. Then have them locate Lancaster, Pennsylvania. Explain that the story takes place in the early days of the white settlement of the area, probably in the mid to late 1700s. At this time, Philadelphia was the largest city in the area. Western Pennsylvania had been partially explored and settled, but the land to the west, where Ohio is today, was still mainly Indian territory. Ask students to use the pictures to compare and contrast the lives of the Indians and the white settlers. Ask which group seems to have the most freedom, and why. Tell students the story is about a young white boy living on the frontier who is raised by Indians. Ask them to speculate about the conflicts that he might have, and what could happen if he were to return to live among the white settlers.

Activity #2

    Distribute the materials students will use in this unit. Explain in detail how students are to use these materials.

    Study Guides Students should preview the study guide questions before each reading assignment to get a feeling for what events and ideas are important in that section. After reading the section, students will (as a class or individually) answer the questions to review the important events and ideas from that section of the book. Students should keep the study guides as study materials for the unit test.

    Reading Assignment Sheet You need to fill in the reading assignment sheet to let students know when their reading has to be completed. You can either write the assignment sheet on a side blackboard or bulletin board and leave it there for students to see each day, or you can "ditto" copies for each student to have. In either case, you should advise students to become very familiar with the reading assignments so they know what is expected of them.

Extra Activities Center The resource sections of this unit contain suggestions for a library of related books and articles in your classroom as well as crossword and word search puzzles. Make an extra activities center in your room where you will keep these materials for students to use. (Bring the books and articles in from the library and keep several copies of the puzzles on hand). Explain to students that these materials are available for students to use when they finish reading assignments or other class work early.

Books Each school has its own rules and regulations regarding student use of school books. Advise students of the procedures that are normal for your school.

Nonfiction Assignment Sheet

Explain to students that they each are to read at least one nonfiction piece at some time during the unit. Students will fill out a nonfiction assignment sheet after completing the reading to help you (the teacher) evaluate their reading experiences and to help the students think about and evaluate their own reading experiences. Topics for research include, but are not limited to, the following suggestions: the history of European colonization in the Americas; the development of English settlements in North America; the customs and life style of any one of the North American Indian tribes from early history through current times; any one of the forced Indian migrations; accounts of white people who lived among the Indians; the history of Pennsylvania or Ohio; groups that are working now to preserve the Native American heritage.

Activity #3

Do a group KWL Sheet with the students (form included.) Students may know something about Conrad Richter and/or *The Light in the Forest* and will have information to share. Put this information in the K column (what I know.) Ask students what they want to find out, and put it in the W column (what I want to find out.) Keep the sheet and refer back to it after reading the book, and complete the L column (what I learned.)

Activity #4

Show students how to preview the study questions and do the vocabulary work for Chapters 1-3 of *The Light in the Forest*. If students do not finish this assignment during the class period, they should complete it prior to the next class meeting.

KWL *The Light in the Forest*

Directions: Before reading, think about what you already know about Conrad Richter and/or *The Light in the Forest.* Write the information in the K column. Think about what you would like to find out from reading the book. Write your questions in the W column. After you have read the book, use the L column to write the answers to your questions from the W column, and anything else you remember from the book.

<u>K</u> What I Know	<u>W</u> What I Want to Find Out	<u>L</u> What I Learned

NONFICTION ASSIGNMENT SHEET *The Light in the Forest*
(To be completed after reading the required nonfiction article)

Name _____ Date _____ Class _____

Title of Nonfiction Read _____

Written By _____ Publication Date _____

I. Factual Summary: Write a short summary of the piece you read.

II. Vocabulary:
    1. With which vocabulary words in the piece did you encounter some degree of difficulty?

    2. How did you resolve your lack of understanding with these words?

III. Interpretation: What was the main point the author wanted you to get from reading his work?

IV. Criticism:
    1. With which points of the piece did you agree or find easy to accept? Why?

    2. With which points of the piece did you disagree or find difficult to believe? Why?

V. Personal Response: What do you think about this piece? OR How does this piece influence your ideas?

LESSON TWO

Objectives
    1. To read Chapters 1-3 orally
    2. To give students practice reading orally
    3. To review the main ideas and events from Chapters 1-3

Activity #1

    Read Chapter 1 out loud to the students and encourage them to follow along in their books. Then have them read Chapters 2-3 out loud in class. You probably know the best way to get readers with your class; pick students at random, ask for volunteers, or use whatever method works best for your group.

Activity #2

    Give students a few minutes to formulate answers for the study guide questions for Chapters 1-3, and then discuss the answers to the questions in detail. Write the answers on the board or overhead projector so students can have the correct answers for study purposes. Encourage students to take notes. If students have purchased their own copies of the book, suggest that they use high lighters in their books to indicate vocabulary words and the answers to study guide questions.

    Note: It is a good practice in public speaking and leadership skills for individual students to take charge of leading the discussions of the study questions. Perhaps a different student could go to the front of the class and lead the discussion each day that the study questions are discussed during this unit. Of course, the teacher should guide the discussion when appropriate and be sure to fill in any gaps the students leave.

LESSON THREE

Objectives
1. To preview the study questions for Chapters 4-6
2. To familiarize students with the vocabulary in Chapters 4-6
3. To read Chapters 4-6
4. To evaluate students' oral reading

Activity #1
Give students about fifteen minutes to preview the study questions for Chapters 4-6 of *The Light in the Forest* and do the related vocabulary work.

Activity #2
Have students take turns reading orally as the others follow along in their books. If you have not yet completed an oral reading evaluation for your students for this marking period, this would be a good opportunity to do so. A form is included with this unit for your convenience.

ORAL READING EVALUATION *The Light in the Forest*

Name_____Class_____Date_____--

SKILL	EXCELLENT	GOOD	AVERAGE	FAIR	POOR
Fluency	5	4	3	2	1
Clarity	5	4	3	2	1
Audibility	5	4	3	2	1
Pronunciation	5	4	3	2	1
_____	5	4	3	2	1
_____	5	4	3	2	1

Total _____ Grade _____

Comments:

LESSON FOUR

<u>Objectives</u>
    1. To check to see that students read Chapters 1-6 as assigned
    2. To review the main ideas and events from Chapters 1-6
    3. To preview the study questions for Chapters 7-8
    4. To familiarize students with the vocabulary in Chapters 7-8
    5. To read Chapters 7-8

<u>Activity #1</u>
    Quiz--Distribute quizzes (multiple choice study questions for Chapters 1-6) and give students about ten minutes to complete them. Have students exchange papers. Grade the quizzes as a class. Collect the papers for recording the grades.

<u>Activity #2</u>
    Give students about 15 minutes to preview the study questions for Chapters 7-8 and do the related vocabulary work.

<u>Activity #3</u>
    Have students read Chapters 7-8 silently for the rest of the period. If students do not complete reading these chapters during this class period, they should do so prior to your next class meeting.

LESSON FIVE

<u>Objectives</u>
    1. To give students the opportunity to practice writing to inform
    2. To give the teacher an opportunity to evaluate each student's writing skills

<u>Activity #1</u>
    Distribute Writing Assignment #1 and discuss the directions in detail. Allow the remaining class time for students to work on the assignment. Give students an additional two or three days to complete the assignment.

<u>Activity #2</u>
    Distribute copies of the Writing Evaluation Form (included in this Unit Plan.) Explain to students that during Lesson Nine you will be holding individual writing conferences about this writing assignment. Make sure they are familiar with the criteria on the Writing Evaluation Form.

<u>Follow-Up:</u> After you have graded the assignments, have a writing conference with each student. (This unit schedules one in Lesson Nine). After the writing conference, allow students to revise their papers using your suggestions and corrections. Give them about three days from the date they receive their papers to complete the revision. I suggest grading the revisions on an A-C-E scale (all revisions well-done, some revisions made, few or no revisions made.) This will speed your grading time and still give some credit for the students' efforts.

WRITING ASSIGNMENT #1 *The Light in the Forest*

PROMPT

You are one of the early settlers in what is now Pennsylvania. You have faced hardships and have had many interesting experiences. Now you are going to write a letter about your life in the New World and send it to your friends in England.

PREWRITING

Before writing, make a word web or outline to help organize your thoughts. Think of the categories you will write about (the geographical features of the area, the weather, the food, the hardships, encounters with the Indians, etc.) Then add descriptive words to each category.

Use information from *The Light in the Forest*, encyclopedias, and other books about the early colonial era to make sure your letter is accurate.

DRAFTING

Make sure you observe the correct format for a letter. Begin your letter with a greeting and a few pleasantries. Then use a separate paragraph to describe each part of your life as an early settler. End with a complimentary closing and your name.

PROMPT

When you finish the rough draft of your paper, ask another student to read it. After reading your rough draft, he/she should tell you what he/she liked best about your work, which parts were difficult to understand, and ways in which your work could be improved. Reread your paper considering your critic's comments, and make the corrections you think are necessary.

PROOFREADING

Do a final proofreading of your paper, double-checking your grammar, spelling, organization, and the clarity of your ideas. You may want to write a final copy of your letter on a paper bag, or make your own writing paper to have your letter look authentic.

WRITING EVALUATION FORM *The Light in the Forest*

Name _____ Date _____ Class _____

Writing Assignment #____ for *The Light in the Forest*

Circle One For Each Item:

Introduction	excellent	good	fair	poor
Body Paragraphs	excellent	good	fair	poor
Summary	excellent	good	fair	poor
Grammar	excellent	good	fair	poor (errors noted)
Spelling	excellent	good	fair	poor (errors noted)
Punctuation	excellent	good	fair	poor (errors noted)
Legibility	excellent	good	fair	poor (errors noted)

Strengths:

Weaknesses:

Comments/Suggestions:

LESSON SIX

Objectives
1. To review the main ideas in Chapters 7-8
2. To preview the study questions and vocabulary for Chapters 7-8
3. To read Chapters 9-11 silently

Activity #1
Ask students to get out their books and some paper (not their study guides.) Tell students to write down ten questions and answers which cover the main events and ideas in Chapters 7-8. Discuss the students' questions and answers orally, making a list on the board of the questions with brief responses. Put a star next to the students' questions and answers that are essentially the same as the study guide questions. Be sure that all the study guide questions are answered.

Activity #2
Tell students to do the prereading and reading work for Chapters 9-11 prior to your next class meeting. Students may use the remainder of this class period to begin working on this assignment.

LESSON SEVEN

Objectives
1. To review the main ideas and events of Chapters 7-11
2. To check to see that the students did the reading assignment
3. To assign the pre-reading, vocabulary, and reading work for Chapters 12-13

Activity #1
Give students a quiz on Chapters 7-11. Use either the short answer or multiple choice form of the study guide questions as a quiz so that in discussing the answers to the quiz you also answer the study guide questions. Collect the papers for grade recording.

Activity #2
Tell students that prior to the next lesson they must have completed the pre-reading, vocabulary and reading work for Chapters 12-13. Give them the rest of the class period to work on this assignment. You may want to allow students who finish early to go to the library and find information for their nonfiction assignments.

LESSON EIGHT

<u>Objectives</u>
      1. To review the main ideas and events from Chapters 12-13
      2. To introduce Writing Assignment #2

<u>Activity #1</u>
      Review the study questions from Chapters 12-13.

<u>Activity #2</u>
      Distribute Writing Assignment #2. Discuss the directions in detail and give students ample time to complete the assignment.

WRITING ASSIGNMENT #2 *The Light in the Forest*

PROMPT

A meeting between the chiefs of the local Indian tribes and the leaders of the white settlers has been called. The topic for the meeting is whether or not to return the captured white settlers to their white families, or to leave them with their new Indian families. The Indians do not want to return their prisoners. The whites want their relatives returned.

In this writing assignment, you are to become either an Indian chief or a white settlers' leader. Your assignment is to write a position paper for your side. The purpose it to persuade your opponents to agree to solve the problem according to your recommendations.

PREWRITING

To begin, decide which side you want to take--the Indians' or the settlers'. On a piece of paper, write the main points, the facts that will support your argument. Decide which points are your strongest ant which of the arguments you will make are weaker. Organize your points from weakest to strongest and jot down anything you can think of which will support or explain your points. You may use the novel *The Light in the Forest*, and outside sources such as other novels about the same topic, encyclopedias, or newspaper articles as references.

DRAFTING

Begin with an introductory paragraph in which you introduce your position. Follow that with one paragraph for each of the main points you have to support your case. fill in each paragraph with examples and facts which support your main point. Then, write a paragraph in which you make your final closing statements.

PROMPT

When you finish the rough draft of your resume, ask another student to look at it. After reading your rough draft, he/she will tell you what he/she liked best about your work, which parts were not clear, and ways in which your work could be improved. Reread your resume considering your critic's comments, and make the corrections you think are necessary.

PROOFREADING

Do a final proofreading of your resume, double-checking your grammar, spelling, organization, and the clarity of your ideas.

LESSON NINE

Objectives
1. To have students revise their first writing assignment papers
2. To give students time to work on their other reading and writing assignments

Activity #1
Call students to your desk (or some other private area) to discuss their papers from Writing Assignment #1. Use the completed Writing Evaluation Form as a basis for your critique.

Activity #2
Students should use this period (when they are not conferencing with you) to work on Writing Assignment #2, revisions of Writing Assignment #1, or their Nonfiction reading assignment.

LESSON TEN

Objectives
1. To do the prereading and vocabulary work for Chapters 14-15
2. To read Chapters 14-15 aloud with a partner
3. To review the main ideas and events from Chapters 14-15

Activity #1
Distribute copies of the vocabulary worksheet and give students about ten minutes to complete it.

Activity #2
Go over the Study Guide questions for Chapters 14-15.

Activity #3
Explain to the students that they will be doing partner reading. Assign partners, or let the students choose their own (whichever works best for your class.) Students will take turns reading aloud in a low voice to each other.

Activity #4
Allow student partners to work together to answer the Study Guide questions. Review the answers with the students.

LESSON ELEVEN

Objective

To discuss *The Light in the Forest* on interpretive and critical levels

Activity #1

Choose the questions from the Extra Discussion Questions/Writing Assignments which seem most appropriate for your students. A class discussion of these questions is most effective of students have been given the opportunity to formulate answers to the questions prior to the discussion. To this end, you may either have all the students formulate answers to all the questions, divide your class into groups and assign one or more questions to each group, or you could assign one question to each student in your class. The option you choose will make a difference in the amount of class time needed for this activity.

Activity #2

After students have had ample time to formulate answers to the questions, begin your class discussion of the questions and the ideas presented by the questions. Be sure students take notes during the discussion so they have information to study for the unit test.

LESSON TWELVE

Objective

1. To give students the opportunity to express their personal opinions in writing
2. To give the teacher the opportunity to evaluate the students' writing skills

Activity

Distribute Writing Assignment #3. Discuss the directions in detail and give students ample time to complete the assignment. Give students the rest of this period to begin working on Writing Assignment #3.

LESSON THIRTEEN

Objective

1. To give students the opportunity to do library research for their nonfiction assignments

Activity

Take students to the school library to work on their nonfiction assignments. Students who have finished working on their nonfiction assignments can use the period to read or revise writing assignments.

EXTRA WRITING ASSIGNMENT/DISCUSSION QUESTIONS
The Light in the Forest

Interpretation

1. From what point of view is the book written? How does this affect our understanding of the story?

2. What insights into the life of the Indian tribes during the early American settlement does the author provide?

3. What insights into the life of the early American settlers does the author provide?

4. What are the main conflicts in the story, and how are they resolved?

5. Based on the facts in the story, can you tell approximately in what year the story takes place? Is this important? If you can't tell the approximate time from the story, how can you find that information?

6. What are the main themes in the novel?

7. What is the setting of the novel? How important is the setting? Why?

8. Explain the role of each of these characters: Del, True Son, Cuyloga, Harry Butler, Uncle Wilse, and Half Arrow.

9. Which of the characters was most developed?

10. Which of the characters was least developed?

11. Why did Cuyloga send presents to True Son via Half Arrow instead of giving him the things before he left to go with the white men?

12. What did Little Crane mean when he said the whites were not an original people?

13. How did True Son feel when he first saw the land the whites had developed by destroying the Indian forests?

14. What was the significance of True Son's dream about his white family?

15. Why did True Son warn the white people on the flatboat?

16. Why did True Son feel and act differently toward Gordie than he did to the rest of his white family?

17. What else could True Son have done instead of warning the white people on the flatboat?

18. What other approach could the Butler family have taken to reassimilate True Son to their way of life?

Critical

19. Explain the significance of the title *The Light in the Forest*.

20. Discuss the irony in Parson Elder's conversation with True Son.

21. How were Bejance and True Son alike? How were they different?

22. Explain how True Son changes over the course of the novel.

23. Do any of the other characters change over the course of the novel? Who changes, and how do they change?

24. Are the characters and events in the book believable?

25. Where is the climax of the story? Defend your answer.

Personal Response

26. Did you enjoy reading *The Light in the Forest*? Why or why not?

27. Have you read any other books about this era in American history? How were they like this one? How were they different?

28. How did you feel about Cuyloga and Harry Butler as fathers?

29. Have you read any other works by Conrad Richter? Did you like them? If you have read several, which was your favorite?

30. If you were in True Son's position, what would you want to do? Why?

31. How does your own ethnic background and experience influence your understanding of and opinion of this book?

QUOTATIONS *The Light in the Forest*

Discuss the significance of the following quotations.

1. "The boy was about fifteen years old. He tried to stand very straight and still when he heard the news, but inside of him everything had gone black."

2. "Now go like an Indian, True Son," he said in a low, stern voice. "Give me no more shame."

3. "But I was plumb wrong. They hated to give them up all right. But they hated worse to see a white man's town a settin' there on the banks of their own river. They hated like poison the sight of our tents and redoubts. They couldn't wait to clear out or axes from cuttin' down their Injun woods and our cattle from eatin' the grass on their river bottoms. They were scared we were takin' over the country. So they started fetchin' in their white relations."

4. "You've been away from us a long time," Del soothed him. "When you're back in our country a while, you'll get used to us."

5. "It is better to wait for your cause to be ripe like a persimmon on the snow before you fight back. True Son. It is wiser to be willing and be alive than be defiant and be dead so your father and mother and sisters have to mourn you."

6. "Well, once an Indian always an Indian. You can make an Indian out of a white man but you can never make a white man out of an Indian."

7. "No, I'm never free from white folks," the Negro assented. "And neither are you and your brother. Every day they drop another fine strap around you. Little by little they buckle you up so you don't feel it too much at one time. sooner or later they have you all hitched up, but you've got so used to it by that time you hardly know it. You eat with a fork and spoon. You sleep in a bed. You own a house and a piece of land and pays taxes. You hoe all day in the cornfield and toil and sweat a diggin' up stumps. Piece by piece you get broke in to livin' in a stall by night, and by day pullin' burdens that mean nothin' to the soul inside of you."

8. "Perhaps the Ruler of Heaven and Earth had imprisoned him to make him value freedom when he got out."

9. "Better your horse dead than the favorite young ones of the poor Indian," the boy asserted.

10. "It was curious how at such a time in the shadow of death all the belongings of the helpless victim affected a father to a degree he dared not speak of even to his wife."

11. "Joy rose in him at the thought that he couldn't go back, for, if he did, they would surely put him and Half Arrow in irons."

12. "Cousin. You have been too long among the whites. They have corrupted your thinking. You have believed their false claims that justify their plunder and pillage. Now, all we Indians know it its not stealing to take back from the whites what they took from us."

13. "The last time I saw it, I was heavy and a prisoner," he said. "Now I go light and free."

14. "*Elke!* Do you live yet, True Son! And are you come home to stay?" His father said, breathing heavily.

15. "True Son felt a savage sweetness he had never known before. He saw before his eyes a redness that colored all things like blood. He tasted a violence wilder than any root or game. Then Thitpan led the way out of the council house, followed bin a single line by the rest."

16. "When will the white man learn!" he muttered. "He says to the Indian, brother, have peace. The Indian buries the tomahawk. He hides it deep under a stump. He believes his brother, the white man. He visits his brother, the white man. Then his brother, the white man, murders him, a guest under his roof. He thinks no more of it than killing a snake in his cabin. The white man talks to other Indians. He says, brother, what's the matter? Why do you go to war? Why dig up the tomahawk? *Ekih!* The white man is a strange creature of the Almighty. He is hard to fathom. How can you reason with him? He is like a spoiled child without instruction. He has no understanding of good and evil."

17. "For the moment he forgot who and where he was. He was conscious only of this child so like Gordie coming closer and closer to the unseen rifles and tomahawks of his companions."

18. "How could life mean anything to you if already your people had killed you in their minds?"

19. "Never did I think that you would turn against me and that I would have to send you back to your white people. All this time I looked on you as an Indian. I leaned on you as a staff. Now it is broken."

20. "Then who is my father?" the boy cried in despair and turned quickly to hide the blinding wetness in his eyes.

WRITING ASSIGNMENT # 3 *The Light in the Forest*.

PROMPT

One of the themes of *The Light in the Forest* is that although we, as Americans, have a large amount of freedom, we have also lost a lot of our freedom to civilization. Bejance, the slave, discusses this theme with True Son and Gordie in Chapter 8. True Son makes observations about it throughout the novel.

Your assignment is to write your own ideas about freedom, and what it means to you.

PREWRITING

Before writing, take time to think about the concept of freedom. If you have lived or traveled in another country, compare the freedoms you had there with what you have in the United States. Then make a word web and jot down all the words you can think of that relate to freedom. Consult a thesaurus for synonyms for the words you have and add these words to your list. You may also want to look up the dictionary definition of the word "freedom."

DRAFTING

Organize your ideas and group similar concepts together. Then begin writing. Start with an introductory paragraph in which you write your definition of freedom. In the following paragraphs, give examples of freedom. Also include any limitations you feel you have because of freedom in other areas. If you refer to outside sources, make sure to use footnotes and credit the sources at the end of your paper. Conclude with a brief summary of your ideas.

PROMPT

When you finish the rough draft, ask another student to look at it. You may even want to read it aloud for the student. After reading/listening, he/she should tell you what he/she liked best about your paper, which parts were difficult to understand or needed more information, and ways in which your work could be improved. Reread your paper considering your critic's comments, and make the corrections you think are necessary.

PROOFREADING

Do a final proofreading of your paper, double-checking your grammar, spelling, organization, and the clarity of your ideas.

LESSON FOURTEEN

Objective
    To review all of the vocabulary work done in this unit

Activity
    Choose one (or more) of the following vocabulary review activities and spend your class period as directed in the activity. Some of the materials for these review activities are located in the Vocabulary Resource section of this unit.

VOCABULARY REVIEW ACTIVITIES

1. Divide your class into two teams and have an old-fashioned spelling or definition bee.

2. Give each of your students (or students in groups of two, three or four) a Vocabulary Word Search Puzzle for *The Light in the Forest*. The person (group) to find all of the vocabulary words in the puzzle first wins.

3. Give students a Vocabulary Word Search Puzzle for *The Light in the Forest* without the word list. The person or group to find the most vocabulary words in the puzzle wins.

4. Use a Vocabulary Crossword Puzzle for *The Light in the Forest*. Put the puzzle onto a transparency on the overhead projector (so everyone can see it), and do the puzzle together as a class.

5. Give students a Vocabulary Matching Worksheet for *The Light in the Forest* to do.

6. Divide your class into two teams. Use the vocabulary words from *The Light in the Forest* with their letters jumbled as a word list. Student 1 from Team A faces off against Student 1 from Team B. You write the first jumbled word on the board. The first student (1A or 1B) to unscramble the word wins the chance for his/her team to score points. If 1A wins the jumble, go to student 2A and give him/her a definition. He/she must give you the correct spelling of the vocabulary word which fits that definition. If he/she does, Team A scores a point, and you give student 3A a definition for which you expect a correctly spelled matching vocabulary word. Continue giving Team A definitions until some team member makes an incorrect response. An incorrect response sends the game back to the jumbled-word face off, this time with students 2A and 2B. Instead of repeating giving definitions to the first few students of each team, continue with the student after the one who gave the last incorrect response on the team. For example, if Team B wins the jumbled-word face-off, and student 5B gave the last incorrect answer for Team B, you would start this round of definition questions with student 6B, and so on. The team with the most points wins!

LESSON FIFTEEN

Objectives
1. To study in more detail some of the characters in *The Light in the Forest*
2. To re-enact scenes from *The Light in the Forest*

Activity #1
Divide your class into groups, one for each of the following: True Son, Cuyloga, Harry Butler, Uncle Wilse, Myra Butler, Aunt Kate, Del Hardy, Half Arrow, and Thitpan. Each group should write down the characteristics of the character they are assigned. Then they should confer and form an opinion about that character.

Activity #2
Have a spokesperson from each group report the group's findings. Encourage the rest of the class to ask questions. If they disagree with the opinions of the reporting group, they must present evidence from the book to support their argument. You may want to have a large piece of paper on the chalkboard or bulletin board. Put the name of each of the characters at the top of the chart. Have a writer from each group record the characteristics the group has noted. Students with artistic ability could draw their interpretations of what the characters look like.

Activity #3
Divide students into small groups. Have each group choose a favorite scene from the novel to re-enact. Give students ten or fifteen minutes to rehearse. As each group presents, have the rest of the class watch and try to identify the scene.

LESSON SIXTEEN

Objectives
1. To widen the breadth of students' knowledge about the topics discussed or touched upon in *The Light in the Forest*
2. To check students' non-fiction assignments

Activity
Ask each student to give a brief oral report about the nonfiction work he/she read for the nonfiction assignment. Your criteria for evaluating this report will vary depending on the level of your students. You may wish for students to give a complete report without using notes of any kind, or you may want students to read directly from a written report, or you may want to do something in between these two extremes. Just make students aware of your criteria in ample time for them to prepare their reports. Start with one student's report, After that, ask if anyone else in the class has read on a topic related to the first student's report. If no one has, choose another student at random. After each report, be sure to ask if anyone has a report related to the one just completed. That will help keep a continuity during the discussion of the reports.

LESSON SEVENTEEN

Objective
To review the main ideas presented in *The Light in the Forest*

Activity #1
Choose one of the review games/activities included in the packet and spend your class period as outlined there.

Activity #2
Remind students of the date for the Unit Test. Stress the review of the Study Guides and their class notes as a last minute, brush-up review for homework.

REVIEW GAMES / ACTIVITIES

1. Ask the class to make up a unit test for *The Light in the Forest*. The test should have 4 sections: multiple choice, true/false, short answer and essay. Students may use 1/2 period to make the test, including a separate answer sheet, and then swap papers and use the other 1/2 class period to take a test a classmate has devised. (open book)

2. Take 1/2 period for students to make up true and false questions (including the answers). Collect the papers and divide the class into two teams. Draw a big tic-tac-toe board on the chalk board. Make one team X and one team O. Ask questions to each side, giving each student one turn. If the question is answered correctly, that student's team's letter (X or O) is placed in the box. If the answer is incorrect, no mark is placed in the box. The object is to get three marks in a row like tic-tac-toe. You may want to keep track of the number of games won for each team.

3. Take 1/2 period for students to make up questions (true/false and short answer). Collect the questions. Divide the class into two teams. You'll alternate asking questions to individual members of teams A & B (like in a spelling bee). The question keeps going from A to B until it is correctly answered, then a new question is asked. A correct answer does not allow the team to get another question. Correct answers are +2 points; incorrect answers are -1 point.

4. Allow students time to quiz each other (in pairs) from their study guides and class notes.

5. Give students a *The Light in the Forest* crossword puzzle to complete.

REVIEW GAMES / ACTIVITIES

6. Divide your class into two teams. Use *The Light in the Forest* crossword words with their letters jumbled as a word list. Student 1 from Team A faces off against Student 1 from Team B. You write the first jumbled word on the board. The first student (1A or 1B) to unscramble the word wins the chance for his/her team to score points. If 1A wins the jumble, go to student 2A and give him/her a clue. He/she must give you the correct word which matches that clue. If he/she does, Team A scores a point, and you give student 3A a clue for which you expect another correct response. Continue giving Team A clues until some team member makes an incorrect response. An incorrect response sends the game back to the jumbled-word face off, this time with students 2A and 2B. Instead of repeating giving clues to the first few students of each team, continue with the student after the one who gave the last incorrect response on the team.

7. Take on the persona of "The Answer Person." Allow students to ask any question about the book. Answer the questions, or tell students where to look in the book to find the answer.

8. Students may enjoy playing charades with events from the story. Select a student to start. Give him/her a card with a scene or event from the story. Allow the players to use their books to find the scene being described. The first person to guess each charade performs the next one.

9. Play a categories-type quiz game. (A master is included in this Unit Plan.) Make an overhead transparency of the categories form. Divide the class into teams of three or four players each. Have each team choose a recorder and a banker. choose a team to go first. That team will choose a category and point amount. Ask the question to the entire class.(Use the Study Guide Quiz and Vocabulary questions.) Give the teams one minute to discuss the answer and write it down. Walk around the room and check the answers. Each team that answers correctly receives the points. (Incorrect answers are not penalized; they just don't receive any points). Cross out that square on the playing board. Play continues until all squares have been used. The winning team is the one with the most points. You can assign bonus points to any square or squares you choose.

10. Have students complete the last column (What I Learned) of the KWL sheet you distributed in Lesson One. Discuss their answers with the class.

NOTE: If students do not need the extra review, omit this lesson and go on to the test.

QUIZ GAME
The Light in the Forest

Chapters 1-3	Chapters 4-6	Chapters 7-8	Chapters 9-11	Chapters 12-13	Chapters 14-15
100	100	100	100	100	100
200	200	200	200	200	200
300	300	300	300	300	300
400	400	400	400	400	400
500	500	500	500	500	500

LESSON EIGHTEEN

Objective
  To test the students' understanding of the main ideas and themes in *The Light in the Forest*

Activity #1
  Distribute the Unit Tests for *The Light in the Forest.* Go over the instructions in detail and allow the students the entire class period to complete the exam.

Activity #2
  Collect all test papers and assigned books prior to the end of the class period.

NOTES ABOUT THE UNIT TESTS IN THIS UNIT:

There are 5 different unit tests which follow.

There are two short answer tests which are based primarily on facts from the novel. The answer key short answer unit test 1 follows the student test. The answer key for short answer test 2 follows the student short answer unit test 2.

There is one advanced short answer unit test. It is based on the extra discussion questions. Use the matching key for short answer unit test 2 to check the matching section of the advanced short answer unit test. There is no key for the short answer questions. The answers will be based on the discussions you have had during class.

There are two multiple choice unit tests. Following the two unit tests, you will find an answer sheet on which students should mark their answers. The same answer sheet should be used for both tests; however, students' answers will be different for each test. Following the students' answer sheet for the multiple choice tests you will find your answer keys.

The short answer tests have a vocabulary section. You should choose 10 of the vocabulary words from this unit, read them orally and have the students write them down. Then, either have students write a definition or use the words in sentences.

UNIT TESTS

SHORT ANSWER UNIT TEST 1 *The Light in the Forest*

I. Matching/ Identify

____ 1. Cuyloga   A. the boy's white father
____ 2. True Son   B. went with his older brother to see Corn Blade
____ 3. Uncle Wilse   C. sacrificed Indian lives to save his favorite horse
____ 4. Harry Butler   D. betrayed his Indian tribe
____ 5. Gordie   E. the boy's white name
____ 6. Half Arrow   F. translator and guard
____ 7. Del Hardy   G. captured and raised a white boy
____ 8. Aunt Kate   H. accompanied his cousin on his journeys
____ 9. Parson Elder   I. took the boy's Indian clothes away from him
____ 10 John Cameron Butler J. killed and scalped Little Crane

II. Short Answer

1. What news did True Son hear at the opening of the story? How did he feel about it? What did he do to show how he felt?

2. What observations did True Son, Half Arrow, and Little Crane make about the white men?

Short Answer Unit Test 1 *The Light in the Forest*

3. Summarize the discussions True Son had with Uncle Wilse and Uncle George on the afternoon that they met.

4. How did True Son feel about living with his white family again? What did he do about the situation?

5. Describe the parting scene at the end of the novel between Cuyloga and True Son. Include the events that led up to it.

Short Answer Unit Test 1 *The Light in the Forest*

6. What were Dr. Childsley's thoughts about True Son's illness?

7. Why did Cuyloga think True Son should accompany him and the other men on their raid?

DISCUSS THE SIGNIFICANCE OF THE FOLLOWING QUOTATIONS.
8. "True Son felt a savage sweetness he had never known before. He saw before his eyes a redness that colored all things like blood. He tasted a violence wilder than any root or game. Then Thitpan led the way out of the council house, followed bin a single line by the rest.

Short Answer Unit Test 1 *The Light in the Forest*

9. "No, I'm never free from white folks," the Negro assented. "And neither are you and your brother. Every day they drop another fine strap around you. Little by little they buckle you up so you don't feel it too much at one time. sooner or later they have you all hitched up, but you've got so used to it by that time you hardly know it. You eat with a fork and spoon. You sleep in a bed. You own a house and a piece of land and pays taxes. You hoe all day in the cornfield and toil and sweat a diggin' up stumps. Piece by piece you get broke in to livin' in a stall by night, and by day pullin' burdens that mean nothin' to the soul inside of you."

10. "But I was plumb wrong. They hated to give them up all right. But they hated worse to see a white man's town a settin' there on the banks of their own river. They hated like poison the sight of our tents and redoubts. They couldn't wait to clear out or axes from cuttin' down their Injun woods and our cattle from eatin' the grass on their river bottoms. They were scared we were takin' over the country. So they started fetchin' in their white relations."

Short Answer Unit Test 1 *The Light in the Forest*

III. Essay

    What are the main conflicts in the story, and how are they resolved?

Short Answer Unit Test 1 *The Light in the Forest*

IV. Vocabulary

Listen to the vocabulary words and spell them. After you have spelled all the words, go back and write down the definitions.

WORD   **DEFINITION**

1. _____ _____
2. _____ _____
3. _____ _____
4. _____ _____
5. _____ _____
6. _____ _____
7. _____ _____
8. _____ _____
9. _____ _____
10. _____ _____
11. _____ _____
12. _____ _____
13. _____ _____
14. _____ _____
15. _____ _____
16. _____ _____
17. _____ _____
18. _____ _____
19. _____ _____
20. _____ _____

ANSWER KEY SHORT ANSWER UNIT TEST 1 *The Light in the Forest*

I. Matching/ Identify

G	1.	Cuyloga	A.	the boy's white father
D	2.	True Son	B.	went with his older brother to see Corn Blade
J	3.	Uncle Wilse	C.	sacrificed Indian lives to save his favorite horse
A	4.	Harry Butler	D.	betrayed his Indian tribe
B	5.	Gordie	E.	the boy's white name
H	6.	Half Arrow	F.	translator and guard
F	7.	Del Hardy	G.	captured and raised a white boy
I	8.	Aunt Kate	H.	accompanied his cousin on his journeys
C	9.	Parson Elder	I.	took the boy's Indian clothes away from him
E	10	John Cameron Butler	J.	killed and scalped Little Crane

II. Short Answer

1. What news did True Son hear at the opening of the story? How did he feel about it? What did he do to show how he felt?

    He heard that the white prisoners the Indians had been capturing for many years were to be given back to the white people. He didn't want to give up his Indian life. He ran away from the village, blackened his face, and hid in a hollow tree.

2. What observations did True Son, Half Arrow, and Little Crane make about the white men?
    Little Crane said they acted queerly because they were not an original people. They were foolish and troublesome because they were a mixed people, with different colored hair and dyes. They needed a Good Book from the Great Being to teach them good and bad. Half Arrow thought they were all near-sighted because they crowd close to stare at Indians. True Son thought they were hard of hearing because they talked so loudly. Little Crane thought they were young and heedless like children because they accumulated so many possessions. They all agreed that the white men were foolish in the woods.

Short Answer Study Guide Questions with Answers *The Light in the Forest*

3. Summarize the discussions True Son had with Uncle Wilse and Uncle George on the afternoon that they met.

   Uncle Wilse thought True Son still looked more Indian. He said True Son had been brought up as an Indian and would stay that way. When True Son Brought up the Peshtank incident, Uncle Wilse said they deserved it. He said the white men had to make sure the Indian males didn't kill any more whites, and the Indian females didn't have any more children. Later he said he believed in getting rid of vermin.

   Uncle George try to explain to True Son about the relationship between the whites and the Indians. He felt the whites in the wilderness had to take the law into their own hands. If a white man killed an Indian, the trial was usually moved to Philadelphia, where the white man was convicted and hanged. However, if an Indian killed a white man, sympathizers in Bucks County or Philadelphia would shelter the Indian.

4. How did True Son feel about living with his white family again? What did he do about the situation?

   He thought it was like a plague. He eventually wore the white man's clothes because Aunt Kate took away his Indian ones. He tried to ride off to visit Corn Blade, but was stopped by his father and his Uncle Wilse. Eventually he succumbed to a high fever and lay in bed. While he was in bed, Gordie told him that Aunt Kate had seen an Indian staring in the kitchen window. That night, True Son got dressed and climbed out the bedroom window to find Half Arrow waiting for him. They went to Uncle Wilse's cooperage and attempted, unsuccessfully, to kill and scalp him in revenge for his slaying Little Crane. Then they traveled back to their village on the Tuscarawas.

5. Describe the parting scene at the end of the novel between Cuyloga and True Son. Include the events that led up to it.

   True Son betrayed his tribe by warning the white settlers in the flat boat. Disbeliever put charcoal on one side of True Son's face and white clay on the other to signify that the council was undecided about what to do with him. The charcoal signified death and the clay signified life. When it was his turn to vote, Cuyloga took a stick from the fire and blackened his entire face. He told the others that he was responsible for True Son's bad instruction, and should be burned as well. Then he told True Son his heart and head were Indian, but his blood was still thin like the whites. He said he would take True Son to a white man's road, and they would part there. After that, they would no longer be father and son. When they reached the white man's trail, True Son asked his father to say good- by. Cuyloga replied that enemies did not say good by, that they were no longer father and son. True Son asked who his father was, but received no answer

6. **What were Dr. Childsley's thoughts about True Son's illness?**
   He was not able to diagnose it. He thought it was some Indian ailment that white doctors didn't know about. He thought the fever was probably a result of True Son's long and unhappy captivity.

7. **Why did Cuyloga think True Son should accompany him and the other men on their raid?**
   He told his wife the other warriors would think True Son was unwilling to fight against his white people if he did not go with them on the raid.

Discuss the significance of the following quotations.

8. "True Son felt a savage sweetness he had never known before. He saw before his eyes a redness that colored all things like blood. He tasted a violence wilder than any root or game. Then Thitpan led the way out of the council house, followed bin a single line by the rest.
   Thitpan called for revenge for the death of his brother, Little Crane. Cuyloga agreed that True Son should be a member of the war party. The men sang war songs and made death noises. This stirred the new feelings in True Son.

9. "No, I'm never free from white folks," the Negro assented. "And neither are you and your brother. Every day they drop another fine strap around you. Little by little they buckle you up so you don't feel it too much at one time. sooner or later they have you all hitched up, but you've got so used to it by that time you hardly know it. You eat with a fork and spoon. You sleep in a bed. You own a house and a piece of land and pays taxes. You hoe all day in the cornfield and toil and sweat a diggin' up stumps. Piece by piece you get broke in to livin' in a stall by night, and by day pullin' burdens that mean nothin' to the soul inside of you."
   Bejance, the Negro slave, was talking to True Son about their lives among the whites.

10. "But I was plumb wrong. They hated to give them up all right. But they hated worse to see a white man's town a settin' there on the banks of their own river. They hated like poison the sight of our tents and redoubts. They couldn't wait to clear out or axes from cuttin' down their Injun woods and our cattle from eatin' the grass on their river bottoms. They were scared we were takin' over the country. So they started fetchin' in their white relations."
    Del was talking about the returning of the white captives to their white families after they had been living with the Indians. He said that many of the white captives didn't want to go back to their white families. The Indians thought of their captives as families, and didn't want to give them up.

SHORT ANSWER UNIT TEST 2 *The Light in the Forest*

I. Matching/Identify

_____ 1. Thitpan   A. went with his older brother to see Corn Blade
_____ 2. Half Arrow   B. also known as John Cameron Butler
_____ 3. Harry Butler   C. accompanied his cousin on his journeys
_____ 4. Uncle Wilse   D. sacrificed Indian lives to save his favorite horse
_____ 5. Cuyloga   E. killed and scalped Little Crane
_____ 6. True Son   F. wanted revenge for his brother's death
_____ 7. Aunt Kate   G. interpreter and guard
_____ 8. Parson Elder   H. took a white boy and raised him as his own
_____ 9. Gordie   I. took the boy's Indian clothes away
_____ 10 Del Hardy   J. the boy's white father

II. Short Answer

1. Summarize the visit between Parson Elder and True Son.

2 How was True Son "thrice imprisoned?"

Short Answer Unit Test 2 *The Light in the Forest*

3. What news did True Son hear at the opening of the story? How did he feel about it? What did he do to show how he felt?

4. Describe the parting scene at the end of the novel between Cuyloga and True Son. Include the events that led up to it.

5. Describe True Son's escape from the Butler home. Include events from the time he leaves the home until he is back with his Indian family.

6. What helped to keep True Son's spirits up along the journey to his white home?

Short Answer Unit Test 2 *The Light in the Forest*

7. What was the conflict between Thitpan and True Son?

Discuss the significance of the following quotations.
8. "How could life mean anything to you if already your people had killed you in their minds?"

9. "It was curious how at such a time in the shadow of death all the belongings of the helpless victim affected a father to a degree he dared not speak of even to his wife."

10. "The last time I saw it, I was heavy and a prisoner," he said. "Now I go light and free."

Short Answer Unit Test 2 *The Light in the Forest*

III. Essay
    What are the main themes in the novel?

Short Answer Unit Test 2 *The Light in the Forest*

IV. Vocabulary

Listen to the vocabulary words and spell them. After you have spelled all the words, go back and write down the definitions.

WORD	**DEFINITION**
1.	
2.	
3.	
4.	
5.	
6.	
7.	
8.	
9.	
10.	
11.	
12.	
13.	
14.	
15.	
16.	
17.	
18.	
19.	
20.	

ANSWER KEY SHORT ANSWER UNIT TEST 2 *The Light in the Forest*

I. Matching/Identify

Use this key for Short Answer Unit Test 2 and the Advanced Short Answer Test.

F	1.	Thitpan	A.	went with his older brother to see Corn Blade
C	2.	Half Arrow	B.	also known as John Cameron Butler
J	3.	Harry Butler	C.	accompanied his cousin on his journeys
E	4.	Uncle Wilse	D.	sacrificed Indian lives to save his favorite horse
H	5.	Cuyloga	E.	killed and scalped Little Crane
B	6.	True Son	F.	wanted revenge for his brother's death
I	7.	Aunt Kate	G.	interpreter and guard
D	8.	Parson Elder	H.	took a white boy and raised him as his own
A	9.	Gordie	I.	took the boy's Indian clothes away
G	10	Del Hardy	J.	the boy's white father

II. Short Answer

1. Summarize the visit between Parson Elder and True Son.

    Aunt Kate invited Parson Elder to the house. She felt he was responsible for bringing Johnny home, since he had led the prayers that had been answered. She was not happy with the way Johnny was acting. She wanted the Parson to talk to him. The parson offered True Son a glass of whiskey, which he refused. True Son told the parson the only reason white men gave rum to the Indians was to get them drunk and take advantage of them. When that happened, the Indians got angry and killed the white men. Parson Elder acknowledged that some white traders were evil, but insisted he wanted to be friends with the boy.

    Aunt Kate entered the conversation, saying True Son didn't believe his Indian parents did any wrong, like scalping children. True Son insisted Cuyloga did no such thing, but added that Parson Elder had been one of the leaders of the Peshtank men. Parson Elder defended his actions by saying that even good Christian men got out of hand sometimes. He said he tried to stop the Peshtank men, but the men had threatened to kill his favorite horse if he interfered. True Son replied that it would have been better to lose a horse than the favorite children of the Indians.

    Parson Elder told Myra and Aunt Kate to be patient and guide Johnny, but not to push him. He also said that if Johnny found a pretty girl he would probably settle down.

2. How was True Son "thrice imprisoned?"

   He was imprisoned by being in an alien land, in a Yengue house, and wearing a white boy's clothes.

3. What news did True Son hear at the opening of the story? How did he feel about it? What did he do to show how he felt?

   He heard that the white prisoners the Indians had been capturing for many years were to be given back to the white people. He didn't want to give up his Indian life. He ran away from the village, blackened his face, and hid in a hollow tree.

4. Describe the parting scene at the end of the novel between Cuyloga and True Son. Include the events that led up to it.

   True Son betrayed his tribe by warning the white settlers in the flat boat. Disbeliever put charcoal on one side of True Son's face and white clay on the other to signify that the council was undecided about what to do with him. The charcoal signified death and the clay signified life. When it was his turn to vote, Cuyloga took a stick from the fire and blackened his entire face. He told the others that he was responsible for True Son's bad instruction, and should be burned as well. Then he told True Son his heart and head were Indian, but his blood was still thin like the whites. He said he would take True Son to a white man's road, and they would part there. After that, they would no longer be father and son. When they reached the white man's trail, True Son asked his father to say good- by. Cuyloga replied that enemies did not say good by, that they were no longer father and son. True Son asked who his father was, but received no answer.

5. Describe True Son's escape from the Butler home. Include events from the time he leaves the home until he is back with his Indian family.

   True Son was ill with a fever. The doctor thought it was caused by his long and unhappy captivity. Aunt Kate brought his Indian clothes back into the room, hoping that would cheer him up. Gordie told him Aunt Kate had seen an Indian looking in the kitchen window. He waited until Gordie went to sleep that night, then climbed out the window. He found Half Arrow in the woods.

   They went to Uncle Wilse's cooperage because Uncle Wilse had killed and scalped Little Crane there. They attacked Uncle Wilse and tried, unsuccessfully, to scalp him. Then they went to the Butler's barn and True Son collected the article he had been hiding. The two ran away. They were planning to walk back to their home on the Tuscarawas. When they reached the Alleghi Sipu river Half Arrow stole a boat and they floated in it past Fort Pitt and into the Ohio River. After they passed Fort Pitt hey were not afraid of being discovered by the whites, and became freer and less cautious in their actions. They spent about two months hunting, fishing, and relaxing.

When they reached the Muskingum river they bathed in it. When they reached the village, True Son walked past his sisters and his mother and embraced his father.

6. What helped to keep True Son's spirits up along the journey to his white home?
His cousin, Half Arrow, accompanied him. Half Arrow had also brought True Son's bear skin from his father, new moccasins from his mother and sisters, and parched corn from his uncle.

7. What was the conflict between Thitpan and True Son?
True Son knew that one of the scalps belonged to a child. When he brought the matter up to Thitpan, he was met with disapproval by the others.

Discuss the significance of the following quotations.

8. "How could life mean anything to you if already your people had killed you in their minds?"
True Son had warned the whites on the river boat of the impending ambush. Now the council was deciding what to do with him. He had just realized the seriousness of what he had done.

9. "It was curious how at such a time in the shadow of death all the belongings of the helpless victim affected a father to a degree he dared not speak of even to his wife."
Harry Butler was looking at his son's Indian clothing hanging in the room. True Son was sick with a high fever, and the doctor didn't know how to help him.

10. "The last time I saw it, I was heavy and a prisoner," he said. "Now I go light and free."
True Son and Half Arrow had escaped from the Butler home. They were passing Fort Pitt in their stolen boat.

ADVANCED SHORT ANSWER UNIT TEST *The Light in the Forest*

I. Matching/Identify

1.	Thitpan	A.	went with his older brother to see Corn Blade
2.	Half Arrow	B.	also known as John Cameron Butler
3.	Harry Butler	C.	accompanied his cousin on his journeys
4.	Uncle Wilse	D.	sacrificed Indian lives to save his favorite horse
5.	Cuyloga	E.	killed and scalped Little Crane
6.	True Son	F.	wanted revenge for his brother's death
7.	Aunt Kate	G.	interpreter and guard
8.	Parson Elder	H.	took a white boy and raised him as his own
9.	Gordie	I.	took the boy's Indian clothes away
10	Del Hardy	J.	the boy's white father

II. Short Answer

1. What are the main conflicts in the story, and how are they resolved?

2. Explain the role of each of these characters: Del Hardy, True Son, Cuyloga, Half Arrow, Harry Butler, and Uncle Wilse.

Advanced Short Answer Unit Test *The Light in the Forest*

3. What are the main themes of the story? Give examples from the novel of how they are carried out.

4. What did Little Crane mean when he said the whites were not an original people?

5. Explain the significance of the title *The Light in the Forest.*

Advanced Short Answer Unit Test *The Light in the Forest*

III. Quotations
Explain the importance and meaning of the following quotations.

1. "The boy was about fifteen years old. He tried to stand very straight and still when he heard the news, but inside of him everything had gone black."

2. "It is better to wait for your cause to be ripe like a persimmon on the snow before you fight back. True Son. It is wiser to be willing and be alive than be defiant and be dead so your father and mother and sisters have to mourn you."

3. "Well, once an Indian always an Indian. You can make an Indian out of a white man but you can never make a white man out of an Indian."

Advanced Short Answer Unit Test *The Light in the Forest*

4. "Never did I think that you would turn against me and that I would have to send you back to your white people. All this time I looked on you as an Indian. I leaned on you as a staff. Now it is broken."

5. "For the moment he forgot who and where he was. He was conscious only of this child so like Gordie coming closer and closer to the unseen rifles and tomahawks of his companions."

Advanced Short Answer Unit Test *The Light in the Forest*

IV. Vocabulary

Listen to the vocabulary words and write them down. After you have written down all of the words, write a paragraph in which you use all the words. The paragraph must in some way relate to *The Light in the Forest*.

MULTIPLE CHOICE UNIT TEST 1 *The Light in the Forest*

I. Matching/ Identify

____ 1.   Cuyloga   A.   the boy's white father
____ 2.   True Son   B.   went with his older brother to see Corn Blade
____ 3.   Uncle Wilse   C.   sacrificed Indian lives to save his favorite horse
____ 4.   Harry Butler   D.   betrayed his Indian tribe
____ 5.   Gordie   E.   the boy's white name
____ 6.   Half Arrow   F.   translator and guard
____ 7.   Del Hardy   G.   captured and raised a white boy
____ 8.   Aunt Kate   H.   accompanied his cousin on his journeys
____ 9.   Parson Elder   I.   took the boy's Indian clothes away from him
____ 10   John Cameron Butler   J.   killed and scalped Little Crane

II. Multiple Choice

1. What news did True Son hear at the opening of the story?
   A. The whites and Indians were going to sign a peace treaty.
   B. The white prisoners the Indians had captured were to be returned to the whites.
   C. The Indians were to be relocated to a reservation in the far west.
   D. The leader of his tribe had converted to Christianity and ordered the others to do so.

2. True Son, Half Arrow, and Little Crane made some observations about the white men. Which of the following was **not** one of them?
   A. They acted queerly because they were not an original people.
   B. They were all far-sighted because they stood so far away from the Indians.
   C. They were hard of hearing because they talked so loudly.
   D. The white men were foolish in the woods

3. Uncle George said the whites in the wilderness had to take the law into their own hands. What was his reason for this statement?
   A. The whites were Christians and knew better how to tell right from wrong. They really only wanted to help the pagan Indians lead better lives.
   B. The cities where the judges lived were too far away to do them any good.
   C. The laws in Philadelphia and Bucks County were too sympathetic toward the Indians.
   D. They did not have enough money to pay for an army unit to guard them.

4. How did the author describe True Son's perception of the life and customs of the white man?
    A. It was like a steel trap.
    B. It was like a stone around his neck.
    C. It was like being at the bottom of a well with no way up.
    D. It was like a plague.

5. Describe the parting scene between Cuyloga and True Son.
    A. They both cried and hugged each other. Cuyloga said in his heart he would always be True Son's father. True Son said he would never feel at home among the white men, and would find a way to return to the Indians.
    B. True Son ran away into the woods before his father could say anything. Cuyloga left a gun, a blanket, and white man's clothes for True Son. Then he went back to the war party.
    C. True Son begged Cuyloga not to leave him. Cuyloga replied that he had no choice. If he did not leave the boy, the rest of the men would kill them both. He tried to assure True Son that they were better off this way.
    D. True Son asked his father to say good- by. Cuyloga replied that enemies did not say good by, that they were no longer father and son. True Son asked who his father was, but received no answer.

6. What were Dr. Childsley's thoughts about True Son's illness?
    A. He thought the fever was due to True Son's long and unhappy captivity.
    B. He thought True Son was faking to get attention from everyone.
    C. He thought True Son had eaten some May apples to try and kill himself.
    D. He thought True Son was not used to the good food and water the family gave him.

7. True or False: Cuyloga said True Son should accompany him and the other men so the other warriors would know he was willing to fight against his white people.
    A. True
    B. False

8. Which of the following statements is true about Gordie and True Son?
    A. Gordie was jealous of the attention True Son was getting.
    B. True Son found he could get the adults angry by teasing Gordie.
    C. Gordie asked True Son to take him back to the Indians to live.
    D. They began to develop a relationship of mutual respect and understanding.

9. Describe True Son's reactions when he first met his white father.
   A. True Son turned away and refused to acknowledge the man as his father.
   B. True Son was sure he had nothing in common with the man. He compared the white man unfavorably to his Indian father.
   C. True Son laughed in the man's face and told him that a brave warrior like himself could not possibly be the son of such a cowardly looking man.
   D. True Son immediately saw a resemblance between himself and the white man, but he refused to admit it. He stood and glared at the man.

10. True or False: The "Peshtank story" concerned a group of Conestogo Indians who had converted to Christianity. They were massacred by a group of white men led by Paxton.
    A. True
    B. False

Multiple Choice Unit Test 1 *The Light in the Forest*

III. Quotations

Identify the speaker: A. True Son B. Del Hardy C. Cuyloga
　　　　　　　　　　D. Uncle Wilse E. Bejance F. Half Arrow

1. "But I was plumb wrong. They hated to give them up all right. But they hated worse to see a white man's town a settin' there on the banks of their own river. They hated like poison the sight of our tents and redoubts. They couldn't wait to clear out or axes from cuttin' down their Injun woods and our cattle from eatin' the grass on their river bottoms. They were scared we were takin' over the country. So they started fetchin' in their white relations."

2. "It is better to wait for your cause to be ripe like a persimmon on the snow before you fight back. . . . It is wiser to be willing and be alive than be defiant and be dead so your father and mother and sisters have to mourn you."

3. "Well, once an Indian always an Indian. You can make an Indian out of a white man but you can never make a white man out of an Indian."

4. "No, I'm never free from white folks. "And neither are you and your brother. Every day they drop another fine strap around you. Little by little they buckle you up so you don't feel it too much at one time. sooner or later they have you all hitched up, but you've got so used to it by that time you hardly know it. You eat with a fork and spoon. You sleep in a bed. You own a house and a piece of land and pays taxes. You hoe all day in the cornfield and toil and sweat a diggin' up stumps. Piece by piece you get broke in to livin' in a stall by night, and by day pullin' burdens that mean nothin' to the soul inside of you."

5. "Better your horse dead than the favorite young ones of the poor Indian."

6. "You have been too long among the whites. They have corrupted your thinking. You have believed their false claims that justify their plunder and pillage. Now, all we Indians know it its not stealing to take back from the whites what they took from us."

7. "The last time I saw it, I was heavy and a prisoner," he said. "Now I go light and free."

8. "When will the white man learn!" he muttered. "He says to the Indian, brother, have peace. The Indian buries the tomahawk. He hides it deep under a stump. He believes his brother, the white man. He visits his brother, the white man. Then his brother, the white man, murders him, a guest under his roof. He thinks no more of it than killing a snake in his cabin. The white man talks to other Indians. He says, brother, what's the matter? Why do you go to war? Why dig up the tomahawk? *Ekih!* The white man is a strange creature of the Almighty. He is hard to fathom. How can you reason with him? He is like a spoiled child without instruction. He has no understanding of good and evil."

9   "How could life mean anything to you if already your people had killed you in their minds?"

10. "Then who is my father?"

Multiple Choice Unit Test 1 *The Light in the Forest*

IV. Vocabulary

1.	abhorrence	A.	going beyond what is right or proper; excessively forward
2.	aloofness	B.	menacing; threatening
3.	consolation	C.	to suffer patiently without yielding
4.	debased	D.	dark; gloomy
5.	desolate	E.	great afflictions; suffering
6.	doughtier	F.	barren, lifeless
7.	endure	G.	having little emotion or sensibility; impassive
8.	grimace	H.	relieving the sorrow or grief of
9.	humiliating	I.	a conscious choice or decision
10.	insidious	J.	a feeling of repugnance
11.	ominous	K.	more courageous
12.	ostentation	L.	act of bringing under control; conquest
13.	pallid	M.	facial expression of pain, contempt, or disgust
14.	presumptuous	N.	a destructive, evil influence
15.	pestilence	O.	boastful display meant to impress others; showiness
16.	somber	P.	lowering the pride, dignity, or self-respect of
17.	stolid	Q.	physical or emotional distance
18.	subjugation	R.	intending to trap; treacherous
19.	tribulations	S.	having an extremely pale complexion
20.	volition	T.	lowered in character, quality, or value; degraded

MULTIPLE CHOICE UNIT TEST 2 *The Light in the Forest*

I. Matching/Identify

____ 1. Thitpan   A. went with his older brother to see Corn Blade
____ 2. Half Arrow   B. also known as John Cameron Butler
____ 3. Harry Butler   C. accompanied his cousin on his journeys
____ 4. Uncle Wilse   D. sacrificed Indian lives to save his favorite horse
____ 5. Cuyloga   E. killed and scalped Little Crane
____ 6. True Son   F. wanted revenge for his brother's death
____ 7. Aunt Kate   G. interpreter and guard
____ 8. Parson Elder   H. took a white boy and raised him as his own
____ 9. Gordie   I. took the boy's Indian clothes away
____ 10 Del Hardy   J. the boy's white father

II. Multiple Choice

1. What was Parson Elder's defense of his actions with the Peshtank men?
    A. He believed they were on a holy mission from God and should not be stopped.
    B. They had threatened to kill his wife and children if he did not help them.
    C. The Indians had killed his parents and he wanted vengeance.
    D. They had threatened to kill his favorite horse if he tried to stop them.

2. How was True Son "thrice imprisoned?"
    A. He was in the alien land, Yengue house, and white boy's clothes.
    B. He was chained to the bedpost, the door to his room was barred from the outside, and there was a guard under the window.
    C. He had to eat the white people's food, go to their church, and sleep in a bed.
    D. He had no one to talk to in the Delaware language, he was not able to go outdoors, and he was wearing white men's clothes.

3. How did True Son feel when he found out he was being returned to his white family? What did he do to show how he felt?
    A. He didn't want to give up his Indian life. He ran away from the village, blackened his face, and hid in a hollow tree.
    B. He was happy about it. He started dancing and singing in English.
    C. He was not happy, but he was resigned to it. He packed the things he wanted to take with him, and gave the rest to his sisters and his cousins.
    D. He didn't want to go. He cried and begged Cuyloga not to send him.

Multiple Choice Unit Test 2 *The Light in the Forest*

4. Describe the parting scene between Cuyloga and True Son.
   A. They both cried and hugged each other. Cuyloga said in his heart he would always be True Son's father. True Son said he would find a way to return to the Indians.
   B. True Son ran away into the woods before his father could say anything. Cuyloga left a gun, a blanket, and white man's clothes for True Son. Then he went back to the men.
   C. True Son begged Cuyloga not to leave him. Cuyloga replied that he had no choice. If he did not leave the boy, the rest of the men would kill them both. He tried to assure True Son that they were better off this way.
   D. True Son asked his father to say good- by. Cuyloga replied that enemies did not say good by, that they were no longer father and son. True Son asked who his father was, but received no answer.

5. Which of the following was **not** one of the True Son and Half Arrow's actions after True Son escaped from the Butler home?
   A. They went to the cooperage.
   B. They set the Butlers' house and barn on fire.
   C. True Son collected the article he had been hiding in his father's barn.
   D. They tried to scalp Uncle Wilse.

6. What helped to keep True Son's spirits up along the journey?
   A. He sang traditional tribal songs to himself.
   B. He read a letter Cuyloga had given him just before he left.
   C. His cousin, Half Arrow, accompanied him.
   D. He constantly plotted ways of escaping.

7. What was the cause of the conflict between Thitpan and True Son?
   A. True Son said his father should be the leader of the party since he knew the most about following the trails.
   B. Thitpan wanted True Son to walk ten paces behind the rest of the men because he was white, and not completely one of them. True Son insisted he was completely Indian.
   C. Thitpan wanted his family to get most of the booty. True Son thought it should be divided evenly.
   D. True Son knew that one of the scalps belonged to a child. When he brought the matter up to Thitpan, he was met with disapproval by the others.

8. True or False: True Son failed in his duty. He saw a small boy who reminded him of his white brother, Gordie. He called to the people that they were about to be ambushed and they escaped.
   A. True
   B. False

Multiple Choice Unit Test 2 *The Light in the Forest*

9. How did True Son know when he had entered the land of the white men?
   A. He saw road signs in a language he could not understand.
   B. There was a barbed wire fence across the trail that separated the two sides.
   C. He saw where the Indian forest had been destroyed and the white men's houses and farms built.
   D. There was a fort built on the edge of the white land. The group had to go through the fort and the prisoners had to be searched before they could go any further.

10. True or False: Del Hardy was being sent with the boy as a translator, but True Son suspected he was also being sent to guard him.
    A. True
    B. False

Multiple Choice Unit Test 2 *The Light in the Forest*

III. Quotations

Identify the speaker: A. True Son   B. Del Hardy   C. Cuyloga
                        D. Uncle Wilse   E. Bejance   F. Half Arrow

1. "How could life mean anything to you if already your people had killed you in their minds?"

2. "You have been too long among the whites. They have corrupted your thinking. You have believed their false claims that justify their plunder and pillage. Now, all we Indians know it its not stealing to take back from the whites what they took from us."

3. "Well, once an Indian always an Indian. You can make an Indian out of a white man but you can never make a white man out of an Indian."

4. "When will the white man learn!" he muttered. "He says to the Indian, brother, have peace. The Indian buries the tomahawk. He hides it deep under a stump. He believes his brother, the white man. He visits his brother, the white man. Then his brother, the white man, murders him, a guest under his roof. He thinks no more of it than killing a snake in his cabin. The white man talks to other Indians. He says, brother, what's the matter? Why do you go to war? Why dig up the tomahawk? *Ekih!* The white man is a strange creature of the Almighty. He is hard to fathom. How can you reason with him? He is like a spoiled child without instruction. He has no understanding of good and evil."

5. "Better your horse dead than the favorite young ones of the poor Indian."

6. "But I was plumb wrong. They hated to give them up all right. But they hated worse to see a white man's town a settin' there on the banks of their own river. They hated like poison the sight of our tents and redoubts. They couldn't wait to clear out or axes from cuttin' down their Injun woods and our cattle from eatin' the grass on their river bottoms. They were scared we were takin' over the country. So they started fetchin' in their white relations."

7. "*Elke!* Do you live yet, True Son! And are you come home to stay?"

Multiple Choice Unit Test 2 *The Light in the Forest*

8. "No, I'm never free from white folks. "And neither are you and your brother. Every day they drop another fine strap around you. Little by little they buckle you up so you don't feel it too much at one time. sooner or later they have you all hitched up, but you've got so used to it by that time you hardly know it. You eat with a fork and spoon. You sleep in a bed. You own a house and a piece of land and pays taxes. You hoe all day in the cornfield and toil and sweat a diggin' up stumps. Piece by piece you get broke in to livin' in a stall by night, and by day pullin' burdens that mean nothin' to the soul inside of you."

9. "Now go like an Indian. "Give me no more shame."

10. "Never did I think that you would turn against me and that I would have to send you back to your white people. All this time I looked on you as an Indian. I leaned on you as a staff. Now it is broken."

Multiple Choice Unit Test 2 *The Light in the Forest*

IV. Vocabulary

1. alacrity
2. assented
3. berating
4. condone
5. defiant
6. derision
7. distorted
8. exemplary
9. formidable
10. incredulity
11. miasmas
12. odious
13. precepts
14. purging
15. remuneration
16. sinister
17. solace
18. sullen
19. valor
20. varmint

A. agreed; concurred
B. boldly resisting
C. swamp gases; odors of decaying matter
D. payment
E. brooding; morose; sulky
F. one that is considered undesirable or troublesome
G. purifying; cleansing
H. twisted; misshapen
I. arousing fear, dread, or alarm
J. ridicule
K. courage and boldness; bravery
L. scolding
M. speed or quickness
N. comfort in trouble
O. worthy of being imitated
P. rules or principles
Q. evil
R. to overlook, disregard, or forgive an offense
S. arousing strong or intense dislike or displeasure
T. unbelievable

ANSWER SHEET   Multiple Choice Unit Tests   *The Light in the Forest*

I. Matching

1. _____
2. _____
3. _____
4. _____
5. _____
6. _____
7. _____
8. _____
9. _____
10. _____

II. Multiple Choice

1. (A) (B) (C) (D)
2. (A) (B) (C) (D)
3. (A) (B) (C) (D)
4. (A) (B) (C) (D)
5. (A) (B) (C) (D)
6. (A) (B) (C) (D)
7. (A) (B) (C) (D)
8. (A) (B) (C) (D)
9. (A) (B) (C) (D)
10. (A) (B) (C) (D)

III. Quotations

1. _____
2. _____
3. _____
4. _____
5. _____
6. _____
7. _____
8. _____
9. _____
10. _____

IV. Vocabulary

1. _____
2. _____
3. _____
4. _____
5. _____
6. _____
7. _____
8. _____
9. _____
10. _____
11. _____
12. _____
13. _____
14. _____
15. _____
16. _____
17. _____
18. _____
19. _____
20. _____

ANSWER SHEET KEY   Multiple Choice Unit Test 1 *The Light in the Forest*

I. Matching	III. Quotations	IV. Vocabulary
1. G	1. B	1. J
2. D	2. C	2. Q
3. J	3. D	3. H
4. A	4. E	4. T
5. B	5. A	5. F
6. H	6. F	6. K
7. F	7. A	7. C
8. I	8. C	8. M
9. C	9. A	9. P
10. E	10. A	10. R
		11. B
		12. O
		13. S
		14. A
		15. N
		16. D
		17. G
		18. L
		19. E
		20. I

II. Multiple Choice

1. (A) ( ) (C) (D)
2. (A) ( ) (C) (D)
3. (A) (B) ( ) (D)
4. (A) (B) (C) ( )
5. (A) (B) (C) ( )
6. ( ) (B) (C) (D)
7. ( ) (B) (C) (D)
8. (A) (B) (C) ( )
9. (A) ( ) (C) (D)
10. ( ) (B) (C) (D)

ANSWER SHEET KEY   Multiple Choice Unit Test 2 *The Light in the Forest*

I. Matching	III. Quotations	IV. Vocabulary
1. F	1. A	1. M
2. C	2. F	2. A
3. J	3. D	3. L
4. E	4. C	4. R
5. H	5. A	5. B
6. B	6. B	6. J
7. I	7. C	7. H
8. D	8. E	8. O
9. A	9. C	9. I
10. G	10. C	10. T
		11. C
		12. S
II. Multiple Choice		13. P
1. (A) (B) (C) ( )		14. G
2. ( ) (B) (C) (D)		15. D
3. ( ) (B) (C) (D)		16. Q
4. (A) (B) (C) ( )		17. N
5. (A) ( ) (C) (D)		18. E
6. (A) (B) ( ) (D)		19. K
7. (A) (B) (C) ( )		20. F
8. ( ) (B) (C) (D)		
9. (A) (B) ( ) (D)		
10. ( ) (B) (C) (D)		

UNIT RESOURCE MATERIALS

BULLETIN BOARD IDEAS *The Light in the Forest*

1. Save one corner of the board for the best of students' writing assignments for *The Light in the Forest*. You may want to use background maps of Pennsylvania and Ohio to represent the setting of the novel.

2. Take one of the word search puzzles from the extra activities packet and with a marker copy it over in a large size on the bulletin board. Write the clue words to find to one side. Invite students prior to and after class to find the words and circle them on the bulletin board.

3. Have students find or draw pictures that they think resemble the people in the book.

4. Invite students to help make an interactive bulletin board quiz. Give each student a half-sheet of paper (about 4"x5') folded in half so that it can open. On the outside flap, have each student write a description of one of the characters in the text. On the inside, they will write the name of the character. You can staple or tack these papers to the bulletin board so that the students can read the descriptions and lift the flaps to find the answers.

5. Collect pictures of the area mentioned in the book. If possible, the pictures should reflect the time frame in the book--America between the French and Indian War and the Revolutionary War.

6. Divide the bulletin board into two sections. On one section, post pictures of the life style of the early frontier settlers. On the other side, post pictures of the life style of the Native Americans.

7. Have students design a bulletin board that shows what the land in the Northeastern United States looked like before and after the settlers arrived.

8. Display articles about lost/missing people who are returned to their loved ones.

9. Have students design postcards depicting the settings of the book.

10. Display a large map of Ohio and Pennsylvania and have students mark the route that True Son took on his journeys.

EXTRA ACTIVITIES *The Light in the Forest*

One of the difficulties in teaching a novel is that all students don't read at the same speed. One student who likes to read may take the book home and finish it in a day or two. Sometimes a few students finish the in-class assignments early. The problem, then, is finding suitable extra activities for students.

One thing that helps is to keep a little library in the classroom. For this unit on *The Light in the Forest* you might check out from the school or public library other books by Conrad Richter. There are also many other novels on the same topic that students would enjoy reading. Several journals have critiques of Richter's works. Some of the students may enjoy reading these and responding either in writing or in discussion groups.

Your students who have reading difficulties, or speak English as a second language may benefit from listening to all or part of the book on tape. You may want to record it yourself, or ask some of your more fluent readers to make a tape of the book for the others to use.

Other things you may keep on hand are word search puzzles. Several puzzles relating directly to *The Light in the Forest* are included in the unit. Feel free to duplicate them.

Some students may like to draw. You might devise a contest or allow some extra-credit grade for students who draw characters or scenes from *The Light in the Forest.* Note, too, that if the students do not want to keep their drawings you may pick up some extra bulletin board materials this way. If you have a contest and you supply the prize. You could, possibly, make the drawing itself a non-refundable entry fee.

Have maps, a globe, and travel brochures on hand for easy reference. Travel agencies and automobile clubs are good sources for these materials.

The pages which follow contain games, puzzles, and worksheets. The keys, when appropriate, immediately follow the puzzle or worksheet. There are two main groups of activities: one group for the unit; that is, generally relating to the text of *The Light in the Forest*, and another group of activities related strictly to the vocabulary for *The Light in the Forest.*

Directions for the games, puzzles, and worksheets are self-explanatory. The object here is to provide you with extra materials you may use in any way you choose.

MORE ACTIVITIES *The Light in the Forest*

1. Pick one of the incidents for students to dramatize. Encourage students to write dialog for the characters. (Perhaps you could assign various stories to different groups of students so more than one story could be acted and more students could participate.)

2. Have students design a book cover (front and back and inside flaps) for *The Light in the Forest*

3. Have students design a bulletin board (ready to be put up; not just sketched) for *The Light in the Forest.*

4. Invite a member of a Native American group to talk to the class about their way of life and their concerns.

5. Use some of the related topics (noted earlier for an in-class library) as topics for research, reports, or written papers, or as topics for guest speakers.

6. Help students design and produce a talk show. Choose one of the story incidents as the topic. The host will interview the various characters. (Students should make up the questions they want the host to ask the characters.)

7. Have students work in pairs to create an interview with one of the characters. One student should be the interviewer and the other should be the interviewee. Students can work together to compose questions for the interviewer to ask. Each pair of students could present their interview to the class.

8. Invite students who have read other books by Conrad Richter to present booktalks to the class.

9. Invite students who have read a biography of Conrad Richter to tell the class about his life.

10. Invite someone who has lived in one of the areas mentioned in the book to speak to the class.

11. Have students hold small group discussions related to topics in the book. Assign a recorder and a speaker for each group. Have the speaker from each group make a report to the class.

12. Make "missing child" posters describing Johnny Butler and asking for information about his whereabouts.

13. In the novel, Richter referred to the months of the year by their Native American names. have students make their own descriptive names for the months. Interested students can make illustrations to go along with the names.

14. Have students work in groups to devise a plan to re-introduce True Son to the white way of life.

15. It is not clear what happened to True Son after he left Cuyloga. Have students work in small groups to write a sequel telling what happened to him.

16. A move based on *The Light in the Forest* was made by Walt Disney Films in 1958. It may still be available. Check your school media specialist and local video store.

UNIT WORD SEARCH *The Light in the Forest*

All the words in this list are associated with *The Light in the Forest* with emphasis on the characters and events being studied in the unit. The words are placed backwards, forward, diagonally, up and down. The words used in the puzzle are listed below.

Note: In cases where a name is two words, such as True Son, the words have been run together without a space.

```
G A Z Y D D E X O I W G W E D I D A M U S K I N G U M S E Y V Z E I
G E M I D I H E T I V E Z H C R A M L Q N G L W W O M L E I L T N O
D Z E U I S Q G R A F S Q Y D T G O L L G V J K O J E N X I A I D B
G R R X B B X U H T V J N B U T J P I H E R D E R V G F V K A H P H
G R A V E E N O A B W O V S P H I A A H N G M F E U U A T T V W Y U
A G I Y N L U S L Q V O C T G M I X P Y O F H N E K G N P T R A X V
P Y U F B I F V H E U A L R D Z C T D P Z E N I F N U A Y G O D X P
C J A A I E W R M F R E X L T O Y O P E L V B C S A C M B R N Y T X
N O O V U V B B P A I H N A O R S N Q W V E M D H I W F E P R T T U
K C N G C E E J W T Z W V G F H N Y T A C R D U Z H P L T I O A X I
M D A E J R P A S V A Q N E A J I M W N R I N X A X P U E X J A H R
I L B Z S L S F X P Y Z X F F G O Y A H D D M N P P Y D N X L H Y N
P H F H K T O Q D R M J W Q C H A J T T E R O T A I A R T U M H M B
N C U L E U O N S N B L P Z U N E X Z L M T Y Y K L H K M O E G I V
E N D R R X N G I I E Z S G F B V J J W S S A C B Y M O P X H R V R
Q H N O Z G L L O N Y K T E S L I W A A U M Z N Y D M N A J G V N I
P E N N S Y L V A N I A N Q N J O G A N T G R J G R Z A D O Q K I C
N A P T I H T V O L J B C K O G S Y H D U O K F L A T B O A T K I E
Y H E K U R O N W Y S K U F M Z K G T P C A S R D H B E Y F X L T P
G A T D I B I N Z H O R X H M Q K G O O F G R Z V L E S P X N D I L
Y Z Q L Y J G W J X N Y E P A N E L I N N E L Y H E S F D U R H Q S
X S W V C D Z T D W L U S H E S W Z T J N T I V N D Z T D P X C M Z
```

AASTONAH	FLAT BOAT	OHIO
ALLEGHISIPU	FLOUR	PAXTON
AUNT KATE	GRAVE	PENNSYLVANIA
BEJANCE	HARRY	PLAGUE
CAPTAIN	HOLLOW TREE	QUAQUENGA
CONESTOGO	JANUARY	BOAT
CORNBLADE	LENNILENAPE	THITPAN
DELHARDY	MARCH	TUSCARAWAS
DISBELIEVER	MAYAPPLE	WILSE
ELEVEN	MUSKINGUM	YENGUE
FEVER	NOVEMBER	

CROSSWORD *Light in the Forest*

CROSSWORD CLUES *Light in the Forest*

ACROSS

1. The Month of the First Snow
4. River where boys stole the boat: ___ Sipu
8. Cousin who gave his white man's clothes to True Son
9. Township where True Son was born and massacre took place
11. True Son's older sister
14. Indian rumored to live in the hills: ___ Blade
15. True Son's illness caused by his captivity with whites
17. What True Son's life with the whites felt like to him
18. True Son's white mother
21. Johnny's age when he was taken by the Indians
23. Thitpan had one that belonged to a white child
25. Took True Son's Indian clothes away from him: Aunt ___
26. State in which the Tuscarawas River is located
27. Uncle leader of Paxton boys: killed & scalped Little Crane
30. Interpreter and guard: Del ___
32. Number of years John Butler lived with the Indians
33. Half Arrow's father: ___ Fish
35. True Son's Indian father
36. Cousin who accompanied True Son on his journeys: Half ___
37. Bejance's occupation: ___ maker

DOWN

2. Uncle George ___ tried to explain frontier justice to True Son
3. A Shawano who went on the raid with Thitpan: Cheek ___
4. True Son wanted to eat it to commit suicide: May ___
5. True Son thought sleeping in a bed in a house was like this
6. Yankee: white settlers
7. True Son's white father
10. Where True Son hid when he heard he was to return to the whites
11. The Month of the Shad
13. Captured at 4 years of age & raised as an Indian: ___ Son
14. Was killed and scalped by Uncle Wilse: Little ___
15. The Month When the First Frog Croaks
16. Author
17. Peshtank captain; sacrificed Indian lives to save his favorite horse: ___ Elder
18. River where the boys bathed when they returned to their tribe
19. True Son's white name: ___ Cameron Butler
20. The Month When the Ground Squirrels Begin to Run
22. Dr. Who thought True Son's illness was due to miasmas and captivity
24. Indian name for Paxton
28. A'astonah was True Son's younger ___
29. Tribe of Indians massacred at Peshtank
31. Indian language True Son spoke
34. Thitpan's father-in-law who had only one eye: High-___

CROSSWORD ANSWER KEY *Light in the Forest*

UNIT MATCHING QUIZ 1 *The Light in the Forest*

_____ 1. Alec
_____ 2. Bejance
_____ 3. Disbeliever
_____ 4. hollow tree
_____ 5. November
_____ 6. Paxton
_____ 7. Yengue
_____ 8. John Cameron Butler
_____ 9. A'astonah
_____ 10. Alleghi Sipu
_____ 11. Del Hardy
_____ 12. captain
_____ 13. Susquehanna River
_____ 14. Aunt Kate
_____ 15. ambush
_____ 16. Gordie
_____ 17. Cuyloga
_____ 18. Delaware
_____ 19. January
_____ 20. Fort Pitt

A. Negro slave and basket maker
B. the Month of the First Snow
C. True Son's white name
D. True Son hid here before his return to the whites
E. took True Son's Indian clothes away
F. True Son's Indian father
G. western end of the white settlements
H. True son wore this white cousin's clothes
I. township where Butler family lived
J. True son's younger sister
K. Parson Elder's rank with Paxton boys
L. True Son warned the whites about this
M. Indian language True Son spoke
N. blackened half of True Son's face with charcoal
O. Month when the Ground Squirrels Begin to Run
P. translator and guard
Q. Yankee; white settlers
R. wanted to wear True Son's Indian clothes
S. river where the boys stole the boat
T. white people stole its land from Cuyloga's tribe

ANSWER KEY UNIT MATCHING QUIZ 1 *The Light in the Forest*

H	1.	Alec	A.	Negro slave and basket maker
A	2.	Bejance	B.	the Month of the First Snow
N	3.	Disbeliever	C.	True Son's white name
D	4.	hollow tree	D.	True Son hid here before his return to the whites
B	5.	November	E.	took True Son's Indian clothes away
I	6.	Paxton	F.	True Son's Indian father
Q	7.	Yengue	G.	western end of the white settlements
C	8.	John Cameron Butler	H.	True son wore this white cousin's clothes
J	9.	A'astonah	I.	township where Butler family lived
S	10.	Alleghi Sipu	J.	True son's younger sister
P	11.	Del Hardy	K.	Parson Elder's rank with Paxton boys
K	12.	captain	L.	True Son warned the whites about this
T	13.	Susquehanna River	M.	Indian language True Son spoke
E	14.	Aunt Kate	N.	blackened half of True Son's face with charcoal
L	15.	ambush	O.	Month when the Ground Squirrels Begin to Run
R	16.	Gordie	P.	translator and guard
F	17.	Cuyloga	Q.	Yankee; white settlers
M	18.	Delaware	R.	wanted to wear True Son's Indian clothes
O	19.	January	S.	river where the boys stole the boat
G	20.	Fort Pitt	T.	white people stole its land from Cuyloga's tribe

UNIT MATCHING QUIZ 2 *The Light in the Forest*

____ 1. May apple
____ 2. Uncle Wilse
____ 3. Under-the-Hill
____ 4. Tuscarawas
____ 5. True Son
____ 6. Uncle George
____ 7. Thitpan
____ 8. Quaquenga
____ 9. plague
____ 10. Philadelphia
____ 11. Parson Elder
____ 12. Ohio
____ 13. Muskingum
____ 14. Myra Butler
____ 15. stolen boat
____ 16. March
____ 17. Mechelit
____ 18. February
____ 19. grave
____ 20. Black Fish

A. True Son thought sleeping in a house was like this
B. the Month of the Shad
C. river where boys bathed upon return to tribe
D. True Son's life with the whites felt like this
E. tried to explain frontier justice to True Son
F. put white clay on half of True Son's face
G. True Son wanted to eat it to commit suicide
H. Half Arrow's father
I. big river at Fort Pitt
J. True Son's Indian mother
K. betrayed his Indian people
L. the Month When the First Frog Croaks
M. Peshtank captain; allowed massacre to save horse
N. Paxton leader; killed and scalped Little Crane
O. Little Crane's brother who wanted revenge
P. True Son's older sister
Q. river where Cuyloga's tribe lived
R. True Son's white mother
S. Indians received sympathetic treatment here
T. True Son and Half Arrow's river transportation

ANSWER KEY UNIT MATCHING QUIZ 2 *The Light in the Forest*

G	1.	May apple	A.	True Son thought sleeping in a house was like this
N	2.	Uncle Wilse	B.	the Month of the Shad
F	3.	Under-the-Hill	C.	river where boys bathed upon return to tribe
Q	4.	Tuscarawas	D.	True Son's life with the whites felt like this
K	5.	True Son	E.	tried to explain frontier justice to True Son
E	6.	Uncle George	F.	put white clay on half of True Son's face
O	7.	Thitpan	G.	True Son wanted to eat it to commit suicide
J	8.	Quaquenga	H.	Half Arrow's father
D	9.	plague	I.	big river at Fort Pitt
S	10.	Philadelphia	J.	True Son's Indian mother
M	11.	Parson Elder	K.	betrayed his Indian people
I	12.	Ohio	L.	the Month When the First Frog Croaks
C	13.	Muskingum	M.	Peshtank captain; allowed massacre to save horse
R	14.	Myra Butler	N.	Paxton leader; killed and scalped Little Crane
T	15.	stolen boat	O.	Little Crane's brother who wanted revenge
B	16.	March	P.	True Son's older sister
P	17.	Mechelit	Q.	river where Cuyloga's tribe lived
L	18.	February	R.	True Son's white mother
A	19.	grave	S.	Indians received sympathetic treatment here
H	20.	Black Fish	T.	True Son and Half Arrow's river transportation

JUGGLE LETTER UNIT REVIEW GAME *The Light in the Forest*

MUASHB	AMBUSH	True Son warned the whites against it
NUKTAEAT	AUNT KATE	took True son's Indian clothes
CJEANBE	BEJANCE	Negro slave and basket maker
FACBKISHL	BLACK FISH	Half Arrow's father
ACATNIP	CAPTAIN	Parson Elder's rank with Paxton boys
IHTRERC	RICHTER	author of novel
NBOLADECR	CORN BLADE	Indian rumored to live in the hills
AGULYOC	CUYLOGA	True Son's Indian father
EYLADRDH	DEL HARDY	interpreter and guard
LADEAREW	DELAWARE	Indian language True Son spoke
SEBEDLIVRIE	DISBELIEVER	blackened half of True Son's face with charcoal
LILSEYCDH	CHILDSLEY	Dr. __ thought True Son's illness was due to captivity
EERFV	FEVER	True Son's illness
ROPTITFT	FORT PITT	western end of the white settlements
DGRIEO	GORDIE	wanted to wear True Son's Indian clothes
AGVER	GRAVE	True Son thought sleeping in a house was like this
LAFARWROH	HALF ARROW	cousin who accompanied True Son
ARYRH	HARRY	True Son's white father
NTTLRLECAEI	LITTLE CRANE	was killed and scalped by Uncle Wilse
ASAMCRES	MASSACRE	what the Paxton boys did to the Conestogo Indians
PAYAMPLE	MAY APPLE	True Son wanted to eat it to commit suicide
RYA M	MYRA	True Son's white mother
HOIO	OHIO	Tuscarawas empties into it
LARONPEDERS	PARSON ELDER	sacrificed Indian lives to save horse
POATNX	PAXTON	township where True Son was born
KPETANHS	PESHTANK	Indian name for Paxton
LAPUEG	PLAGUE	True Son's life with whites felt like this
CLAPS	SCALP	Thitpan had one from a white child
PTHIANT	THITPAN	Little Crane's brother
SOTUENR	TRUE SON	captured raised as an Indian
ERGEGO	GEORGE	tried to explain frontier justice to True Son
ILSWE	WILSE	killed and scalped Little Crane
GENUEY	YENGUE	Yankee; white settlers

VOCABULARY RESOURCE MATERIALS

VOCABULARY WORD SEARCH *The Light in the Forest*

All the words in this list are associated with *The Light in the Forest* with emphasis on the vocabulary words being studied in the unit. The words are placed backwards, forward, diagonally, up and down. The clues below the word search will help identify the words.

```
K U N N D Q S S U V I W N U A V G Y X A P C W N Q U A M J C M R Y J
D X Y Y E J A R C R D U K R I R A K O H N L O D X X O L I S M G V D
P F E X S P M K M W X H E T I X V R F R F D U N G A I N A B J O P M
H E R U A S S S V H N M E M A N E U Q W Z U U Y S R P T N C F Y L I
I E U Q B P A C R Y O R A I Q N R Z K P Q M H Y G O U X D N R I G T
M Q D I E K I F O N L C T M I L S X C B H T P D I R L E Y L Q I R U
Z E N T D S M R S B E G W E K I I E B U L U T D K N T A E U O V T T
S X E W M R P T Q S D I S Q I E O J D A O N M W R R X B T T T T B Y
S U O I D O R R A K T S K A P M N K E Q W M S I O P L X V I Q J J I
L Y O Z Q A L P X H H D E S O L A T E A C E R T L I C F C D O A U G
N S T U T K L E V Q B S D I M K S D S C K R S S I I T V F M E N T T
I H S I T I P O S C M P J Y O R Y U H I P I N O I T A T N E T S O O
N Z N G N P V P Y T Q K H P E M F U K X D T U V G R R T A U W H K N
L G T G R N M T Y O R H Y L D F S B I U R O T C Y B E S I R G D B F
W I E C I T A U F U S U A B O X M D P U L R D H I H E U A N F R P R
B E R A T I N G S E E C C C C S N S N J I P T I A Z O G H G E V G
G A P O N C J Z L E K I A W Y K Y S J P T O W X Y C J I D M Y R D T
C X R T K N H M X E R T L A G F E A X W T U P G D O Z D P R I I G I
V L E A G L V R Y X I P Y J M D Z A D Z Q S M Q V J B I X C O K N V
Y D G D X L I S O N G P X N I T A U R D Y A N G L S T S H R Q Q A P
V A R S C G C K G T V E R M I L I O N W U Y Z S Y I E N N R J U P P
B U M E R G G R L Y U X G V J V M Y O U U S V K A A M I Z M M I M G
```

ALACRITY	HUMILIATING	REMONSTRATING
AVERSION	INSIDIOUS	SAPLING
BERATING	LACKEYS	SEINE
CONSOLATION	MERITORIOUS	STEALTHY
DEBASED	MIASMAS	SUFFOCATING
DESOLATE	MOLEST	TAINTED
DISTORTED	ODIOUS	TRUSSED
ENDURE	OSTENTATION	VERMILION
GRIMACE	PRESUMPTUOUS	

VOCABULARY CROSSWORD *Light in the Forest*

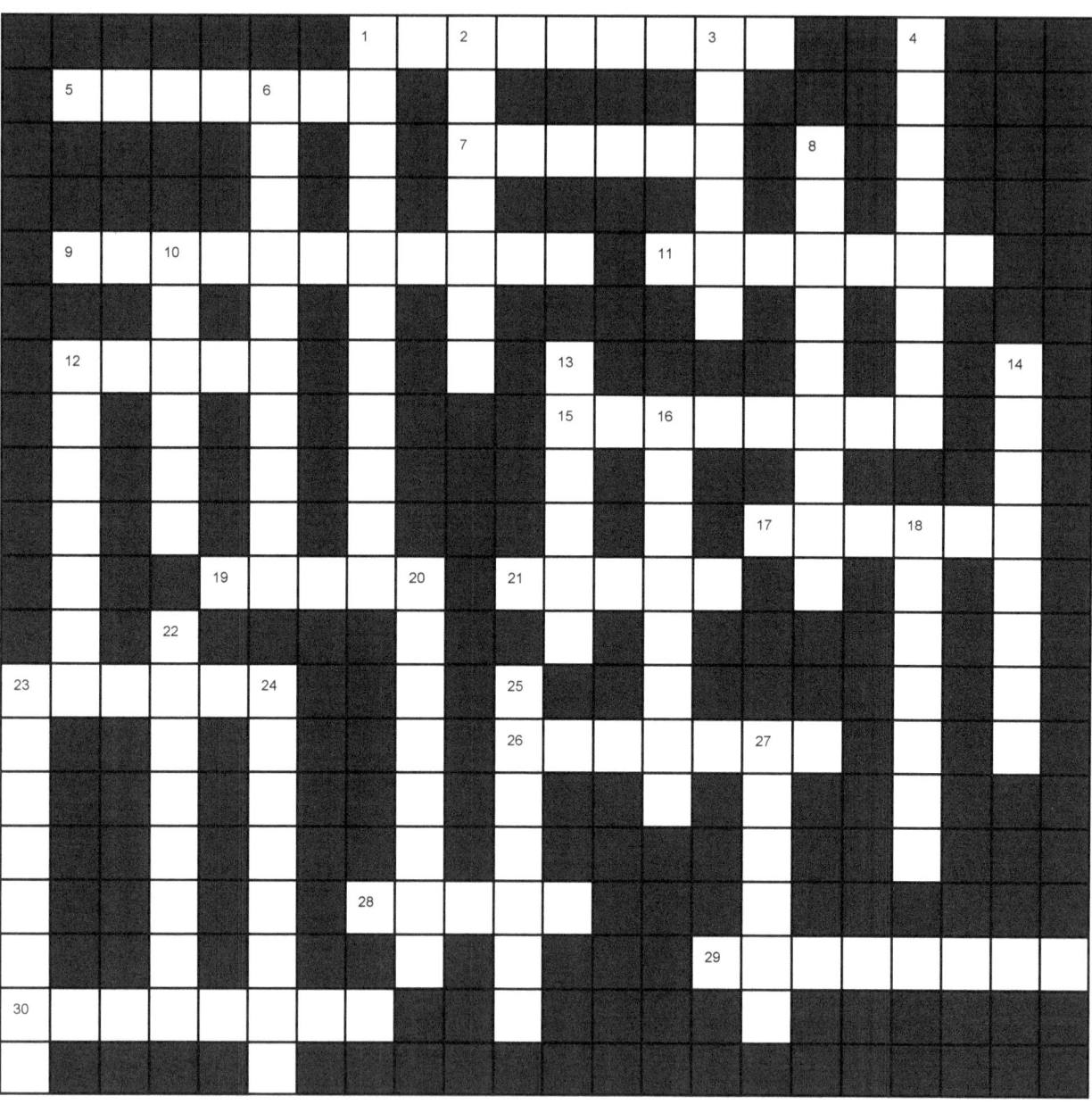

VOCABULARY CROSSWORD CLUES *Light in the Forest*

ACROSS
1 Recognized or comprehended mentally
5 A twisting of the face that expresses pain, contempt, or disgust
7 Having an abnormally pale complexion
9 Temperament; usual mood
11 Tied up
12 Courage; bravery
15 Speed or quickness
17 Excited and often noisy activity
19 Net for catching fish
21 To want something that belongs to another
23 Having or revealing little emotion
26 Pacify; soothe
28 Hang about; wait nearby
29 Ridicule
30 Not paying attention

DOWN
1 The place to which one is going
2 A young tree
3 To suffer patiently without yielding
4 Stinging; capable of burning
6 A feeling of repugnance or loathing
8 Intended to entrap; treacherous
10 Comfort in trouble
12 One that is considered undesirable, obnoxious, or troublesome
13 Understand
14 Having supreme authority
16 Agreed
18 Stained; infected; spoiled
20 Effort
22 Distributed
23 Acting with secrecy to avoid notice
24 Prevented or discouraged from acting
25 Slaves; forced laborers
27 Dark; gloomy

VOCABULARY CROSSWORD ANSWER KEY *Light in the Forest*

							D	I	S	C	E	R	N	E	D			P			
	G	R	I	M	A	C	E		A					N				U			
					B		S		P	A	L	L	I	D		I		N			
					H		T		L					U		N		G			
	D	I	S	P	O	S	I	T	I	O	N		T	R	U	S	S	E	D		
			O		R		N		N					E		I		N			
	V	A	L	O	R		A		G		F					D		C		I	
	A		A		E		T				A	L	A	C	R	I	T	Y		M	
	R		C		N		I				T		S			O				P	
	M		E		C		O				H		S		B	U	S	T	L	E	
	I			S	E	I	N	E		C	O	V	E	T		S		A		R	
	N		A					X			M		N					I		I	
S	T	O	L	I	D			E		L			T					N		A	
T			L		E			R		A	P	P	E	A	S	E		T		L	
E			O		T			T		C			D		O			E			
A			T		E			I		K					M			D			
L			T		S		H	O	V	E	R				B						
T			E		T			N		Y				D	E	R	I	S	I	O	N
H	E	E	D	L	E	S	S			S					R						
Y					D																

VOCABULARY WORKSHEET 1 *The Light in the Forest*

_____ 1. deterred
_____ 2. disposition
_____ 3. doughtier
_____ 4. exultation
_____ 5. filial
_____ 6. heedless
_____ 7. imperial
_____ 8. insidious
_____ 9. meritorious
_____ 10. ostentation
_____ 11. presumptuous
_____ 12. remonstrating
_____ 13. remuneration
_____ 14. sapling
_____ 15. stealthy
_____ 16. stolid
_____ 17. suffocating
_____ 18. tainted
_____ 19. trussed
_____ 20. volition

A. deserving reward
B. pertaining to a son or a daughter
C. killing by taking away oxygen
D. one's usual mood; temperament
E. tied up
F. payment
G. prevented or discouraged from acting
H. going beyond what is right or proper
I. having little emotion; impassive
J. having supreme authority
K. a conscious choice or decision
L. rejoicing
M. stained; infected; spoiled
N. more courageous
O. acting with secrecy to avoid notice
P. not paying attention
Q. pleading in protest
R. a young tree
S. boastful display meant to impress others
T. intended to entrap; treacherous

ANSWER KEY VOCABULARY WORKSHEET 1 *The Light in the Forest*

G	1.	deterred	A.	deserving reward
D	2.	disposition	B.	pertaining to a son or a daughter
N	3.	doughtier	C.	killing by taking away oxygen
L	4.	exultation	D.	one's usual mood; temperament
B	5.	filial	E.	tied up
P	6.	heedless	F.	payment
J	7.	imperial	G.	prevented or discouraged from acting
T	8.	insidious	H.	going beyond what is right or proper
A	9.	meritorious	I.	having little emotion; impassive
S	10.	ostentation	J.	having supreme authority
H	11.	presumptuous	K.	a conscious choice or decision
Q	12.	remonstrating	L.	rejoicing
F	13.	remuneration	M.	stained; infected; spoiled
R	14.	sapling	N.	more courageous
O	15.	stealthy	O.	acting with secrecy to avoid notice
I	16.	stolid	P.	not paying attention
C	17.	suffocating	Q.	pleading in protest
M	18.	tainted	R.	a young tree
E	19.	trussed	S.	boastful display meant to impress others
K	20.	volition	T.	intended to entrap; treacherous

VOCABULARY WORKSHEET 2 *The Light in the Forest*

_____ 1. **kidnapper**
   A. varmint　　B. abductor　　C. covet　　D. meridian

_____ 2. **a feeling of repugnance or loathing**
   A. alacrity　　B. volition　　C. incredulity　　D. abhorrence

_____ 3. **distant physically or emotionally**
   A. aloofness　　B. ominous　　C. defiant　　D. humiliating

_____ 4. **a feeling of extreme repugnance accompanied by avoidance**
   A. ostentation　　B. tainted　　C. aversion　　D. formidable

_____ 5. **relieving the sorrow or grief of**
   A. consolation　　B. appease　　C. purging　　D. remonstrating

_____ 6. **lowered in character, quality, or value**
   A. tainted　　B. deterred　　C. meritorious　　D. debased

_____ 7. **ridicule**
   A. alacrity　　B. derision　　C. valor　　D. pestilence

_____ 8. **twisted; misshapen**
   A. odious　　B. trussed　　C. distorted　　D. filial

_____ 9. **to suffer patiently without yielding**
   A. endure　　B. assented　　C. condone　　D. subjugation

_____ 10. **arousing fear, dread, or alarm**
   A. remonstrating　　B. sinister　　C. stealthy　　D. formidable

_____ 11. **unbelievable**
   A. alacrity　　B. incredulity　　C. fathom　　D. exemplary

_____ 12. **great dislike or abhorrence**
   A. loathing　　B. disposition　　C. tribulations　　D. precepts

_____ 13. **arousing strong dislike or intense displeasure**
   A. berating　　B. purging　　C. odious　　D. presumptuous

_____ 14. **boastful display meant to impress others; showiness**
   A. ostentation　　B. meritorious　　C. destination　　D. bustle

_____ 15. **having an abnormally pale complexion**
   A. vermilion　　B. pallid　　C. pungency　　D. doughtier

_____ 16. **going beyond what is right or proper**
   A. abhorrence　　B. suffocating　　C. presumptuous　　D. insidious

_____ 17. **payment**
   A. remuneration　　B. tribulations　　C. grimace　　D. miasmas

_____ 18. **evil**
   A. bleakly　　B. heedless　　C. desolate　　D. sinister

_____ 19. **comfort in trouble**
   A. aversion　　B. solace　　C. berating　　D. exultation

_____ 20. **great afflictions; suffering**
   A. lackeys　　B. encumbrances　　C. tribulations　　D. aloofness

ANSWER KEY VOCABULARY WORKSHEET 2 *The Light in the Forest*

B 1. **kidnapper**
    A. varmint   B. **abductor**   C. covet   D. meridian

D 2. **a feeling of repugnance or loathing**
    A. alacrity   B. volition   C. incredulity   D. **abhorrence**

A 3. **distant physically or emotionally**
    A. **aloofness**   B. ominous   C. defiant   D. humiliating

C 4. **a feeling of extreme repugnance accompanied by avoidance**
    A. ostentation   B. tainted   C. **aversion**   D. formidable

A 5. **relieving the sorrow or grief of**
    A. **consolation**   B. appease   C. purging   D. **remonstrating**

D 6. **lowered in character, quality, or value**
    A. tainted   B. deterred   C. meritorious   D. **debased**

B 7. **ridicule**
    A. alacrity   B. **derision**   C. valor   D. pestilence

C 8. **twisted; misshapen**
    A. odious   B. trussed   C. **distorted**   D. filial

A 9. **to suffer patiently without yielding**
    A. **endure**   B. assented   C. condone   D. subjugation

D 10. **arousing fear, dread, or alarm**
    A. remonstrating   B. sinister   C. stealthy   D. **formidable**

B 11. **unbelievable**
    A. alacrity   B. **incredulity**   C. fathom   D. exemplary

A 12. **great dislike or abhorrence**
    A. **loathing**   B. disposition   C. tribulations   D. precepts

C 13. **arousing strong dislike or intense displeasure**
    A. berating   B. purging   C. **odious**   D. presumptuous

A 14. **boastful display meant to impress others; showiness**
    A. **ostentation**   B. meritorious   C. destination   D. bustle

B 15. **having an abnormally pale complexion**
    A. vermilion   B. **pallid**   C. pungency   D. doughtier

C 16. **going beyond what is right or proper**
    A. abhorrence   B. suffocating   C. **presumptuous**   D. insidious

A 17. **payment**
    A. **remuneration**   B. tribulations   C. grimace   D. miasmas

D 18. **evil**
    A. bleakly   B. heedless   C. desolate   D. **sinister**

B 19. **comfort in trouble**
    A. aversion   B. **solace**   C. berating   D. exultation

C 20. **great afflictions; suffering**
    A. lackeys   B. encumbrances   C. **tribulations**   D. aloofness

VOCABULARY JUGGLE LETTER REVIEW GAME *The Light in the Forest*

Scrambled	Word	Definition
CAUBTRDO	ABDUCTOR	kidnapper
TAARCIYL	ALACRITY	speed or quickness
SAAPEEP	APPEASE	pacify; soothe
EASTNDSE	ASSENTED	agreed; concurred
GEAIBNTV	BERATING	scolding
ALBKLYE	BLEAKLY	gloomily; cheerlessly
BSUELT	BUSTLE	excited and often noisy activity; a stir
NODOCEN	CONDONE	to overlook or forgive
NOUCSEL	COUNSEL	advice or guidance
VOTEC	COVET	to want something that belongs to another
ADEESDB	DEBASED	degraded
IDAFTNE	DEFIANT	boldly resisting
RDIOSINE	DERISION	ridicule
SEOLAEDT	DESOLATE	barren, lifeless
TEEDREDR	DETERRED	prevented or discouraged from acting
RITSOTEDD	DISTORTED	twisted; misshapen
EHDOGTIRU	DOUGHTIER	more courageous
UEDRNE	ENDURE	to suffer patiently without yielding
AHFOMT	FATHOM	understand
LIIFAL	FILIAL	pertaining to a son or daughter
MRIGAEC	GRIMACE	facial expression of pain
DESELEHS	HEEDLESS	not paying attention
VHERO	HOVER	hang about; wait nearby
PIARLIME	IMPERIAL	having supreme authority
KAYELCS	LACKEYS	slaves; forced laborers
LAGHIOTN	LOATHING	great dislike; abhorrence
LOESMT	MOLEST	to disturb, interfere with, or annoy
IOOUDS	ODIOUS	arousing strong dislike
MOONSUI	OMINOUS	menacing; threatening
LPADLI	PALLID	an abnormally pale complexion
REPTCSEP	PRECEPTS	rules or principles
UPNNECYG	PUNGENCY	stinging; capable of burning
GUINPGR	PURGING	purifying; cleansing
LSGANPI	SAPLING	a young tree
INESE	SEINE	net for catching fish
ENSSIITR	SINISTER	evil
OLACES	SOLACE	comfort in trouble
BOMERS	SOMBER	dark; gloomy
THEALTYS	STEALTHY	acting with secrecy to avoid notice
SOLDTI	STOLID	having little emotion; impassive
LENSUL	SULLEN	brooding; morose; sulky

ANTDIET	TAINTED	stained; infected; spoiled
TSUREDS	TRUSSED	tied up
ROVLA	VALOR	courage and boldness; bravery
RVAINTM	VARMINT	undesirable or troublesome creature
REMILVINO	VERMILION	a vivid red to reddish orange
LIONVTIO	VOLITION	a conscious choice or decision

www.ingramcontent.com/pod-product-compliance
Lightning Source LLC
LaVergne TN
LVHW081536060526
838200LV00048B/2099